'A genuinely fresh contributio
Well researched, well rooted in
the reality of contemporary wo
reading. I usually can't read oth␣␣␣␣␣␣␣␣␣␣␣␣␣
for all kinds of reasons – but from␣ the first page I was
gripped, interested and wanted to read more...so bravo.'

Mark Greene, author of "Thank God it's Monday',
Executive Director of the London Institute for
Contemporary Christianity

'I really enjoyed reading this. It will fill a massive gap in
what is available. The chapter on anger is absolutely bril-
liant. It is realistic, helpful and inspiring. This book is very
much needed and I have found it most illuminating. A lot
of it is applicable to life itself. I recommend it as essential
reading for every working Christian, and for every
Christian minister who seeks to lead and support working
Christians.'

Rev Dr Alison Morgan, author

'I greatly enjoyed reading *90,000 Hours*. It is fresh, very
down-to-earth and full of helpful biblical insight and
wisdom, in an area where there is so little to recommend. In
this unusually frank and realistic account of his own experience of the world of work as a Christian, Rodney Green
opens up a wide range of challenging issues with honesty
and perception. God's Word in Scripture governs both the
principles he explores and their practical application, but
never glibly or simplistically, and always with illumination
and relevance. Full of wise insights, practical realism and
uncommon sense, this is a book for every Christian to read
and ponder, so as to reclaim the vast majority of our
working hours for God and the gospel.'

Rev David Jackman, Proclamation Trust

90,000 HOURS

HOURS

MANAGING THE WORLD OF WORK

RODNEY GREEN

Scripture Union, 207–209 Queensway, Bletchley, MK2 2EB,
England, UK.
Email: info@scriptureunion.org.uk
website: www.scriptureunion.org.uk

© Rodney Green 2002
First published 2002
ISBN 1 85999 594 2

British Library Cataloguing-in-Publication Data
A catalogue record for this book is available from the British Library.

Cover design by David Lund.

Printed and bound in Great Britain by Creative Print and Design (Wales)
Ebbw Vale

To Helen

Love and work are the only things that really happen to us.
Everything else doesn't really matter. *Marilyn Monroe*

In almost thirty years of my professional career, my church
has never once offered to improve those skills which could
make me a better minister, nor has it ever asked if I needed
any kind of support in what I am doing. There has never
been an enquiry into the types of ethical decisions I must
face, or whether I seek to communicate the faith to my co-
workers. I have never been in a congregation where there
was any type of public affirmation of the ministry in my
career. *A sales manager*

Wisdom calls aloud in the street,
 she raises her voice in the public squares;
at the head of the noisy streets she cries out... *Solomon*

In nothing has the Church so lost her hold on reality as in
her failure to understand and respect the secular vocation.
She has allowed work and religion to become separate
departments and is astonished to find that, as a result, the
secular work of the world is turned purely to selfish and
destructive ends and that the greater part of the world's
intelligent workers have become irreligious, or at least unin-
terested in religion. But is it astonishing? How can anyone
remain interested in religion, which seems to have no
concern with nine-tenths of his life? *Dorothy L Sayers*

The race is not to the swift
    or the battle to the strong,
nor does food come to the wise
    or wealth to the brilliant
    or favour to the learned;
but time and chance happen to them all. *Qoheleth*

CONTENTS

The ideas for this book were shaped in collaboration with three friends over a number of discussions for nearly two decades. Ian Angell, Peter Butler, Paul Whitfield and I would often find ourselves from time to time in the pub, chatting, firing off questions, and sharing our perspectives and experiences about work. Occasionally the pub became the venue for an informal dinner and conversation with invited friends, presenting further opportunities for challenging debate. My debt to those three musketeers is incalculable – through them and with them I have learned much about work, leisure and friendship.

INTRODUCTION

90,000. That's the number of hours that the majority of people in the UK in full-time employment (about 45–50 hours per week over 40 years) will probably spend at work (and this includes the hours spent commuting to and from work). In some parts of the world it may be more.

Do you ever wonder if giving 90,000 hours of your life to secular employment – as most Christians do – can be justified in the context of the pressing eternal questions facing humankind?

And what about the other questions? Do you believe that jobs exist in a kind of spiritual hierarchy, with missionaries and vicars at the top, doctors and teachers a little lower down, and ordinary jobs in industry, commerce and government at the bottom? Where does this leave voluntary work, or raising children?

What about work values? Can you differentiate between Christian values and those of an 'honourable' atheist? What is the relationship between employment and work? Why does society appear to esteem full-time, paid employment over very necessary unpaid tasks such as parenting or caring for a loved one at home? What should we think and do about Sunday trading?

Why are stress and conflict so prevalent in the workplace?

How do we handle pressure? Are there unique Christian perspectives on stress? Should a Christian ever express anger in the daily confrontations and frustrations that we all invariably experience at work? When and how is it right to manage anger?

These are the sorts of questions I will be exploring in this book. I should admit, however, that in writing it I was surprised to discover how superficial have been my own ideas on this subject, and how feeble my attempts to relate Scripture to those crucial 90,000 hours of my life. And I have been puzzled by how few Christians seem to share my eagerness to address this. Perhaps many feel that to do so would be to divert us from the 'real' spiritual priorities we face, spiritual priorities which we may confine to the private world of personal religion.

An outside observer could be forgiven for believing that, for the majority of Christians, the Bible only comes into its own after work. They rush back from their day on the 'secular' job, bolt down supper, spend a brief bit of 'quality' time with the children (if they have not already gone to bed), give the spouse a quick peck on the cheek, before heading off into the arena of the 'real job' of the Christian. They may go slightly grey with the strain of trying to fit it all in – the Bible study, prayer, missionary support, neighbourhood evangelism, helping the poor at home and abroad, parish service, the diocesan agendas and leadership meetings – but they live in the hope that all that time spent on church matters will, in the end, somehow leave them spiritually refreshed!

However, some Christians may struggle with a vague sense of unease about how little they really know the Scriptures and apply them to the world that we so often allow to define us and which absorbs so much of our time and energy – the world of work. This sense of unease masks a vacuum in society which is evidence of the divorce, the divorce between theory and practice, faith and works, church and employment, the Bible and public life. It is as if the God of the whole earth – the one Lord, the only Creator and Redeemer of humankind – can be shunted over to rule only in the world of personal religion, with no room for him to interfere in the secular world of public life. When this is allowed to happen unchecked, even personal faith is likely to become increasingly small and irrelevant.

It is assumed that in public life only 'neutral objectivity' holds sway. Yet when we look for this supposed objectivity in contemporary discourse, on matters such as faith schools (which all schools once were in Britain) or whether or not science and religion can mix (nearly all scientists were Christians at one time, and many still are today), we realise that there is indeed a real battle over who is permitted to speak with authority in the public arena. If we really do believe that God speaks afresh to every generation through his Word, why should we not expect him to address the world of work?

I once interviewed an Oxford graduate for a management trainee post. Her application form made several references to her faith. I asked her what biblical insights might have to say to contemporary managers. She referred to humanising influences and differences in motivation. She then added that she could see little difference in practice between the management approaches of most Christians and those of 'honourable' atheists. On another occasion, a Christian management consultant told me flatly that there were no Christian distinctives at work, other than prayer for colleagues and evangelism.

Several times I have been solemnly advised that it is not possible for me to be a follower of Christ and work for the local council! Christians, it was alleged, should keep separate from that world and save their energies for their activities within the community of believers and their family life.

Faith and work operate in two separate dimensions: faith operates in the dimension of personal belief; work operates in the dimension of public reality. The Bible can be helpful in the former but has little to say to the latter.

Is this an adequate view of work or Scripture? If Scripture has so little to say about work, how will we negotiate the rocks and rapids that we encounter as we journey along the river of our working life? How will we cope with relationships with colleagues, income and expenditure, disappointment, unemployment, injustice, health breakdown, exhaustion, stress, ambition, success and retirement? The rocks and rapids of working life have the capacity to buffet and bruise us, maybe even to break us. They come upon us unexpectedly, sometimes all at once and at great speed. The way we deal with them may well determine the direction and character of our whole lives. We need to construct for ourselves a buoyant and substantial raft, made up of the sound wood and strong cords of Scripture, if we hope to navigate through the rough and uncertain waters on our journey of 90,000 hours.

My aim in writing this book has been to build a raft based upon distinctively biblical material. In particular, I will use four 'logs', or themes, that are especially relevant to work: creativity, rest, harmony, and perseverance. These themes should help us to think about our work and may inspire us to transform our 90,000 hours by the 'salt' and 'light' of our faith (Matt 5:13–16). Such building materials may encourage fellow travellers to conceive of ever more ambitious raft constructions, using stronger materials and aiming at an increasing range of exploration.

What about other topics such as evangelism at work, workplace Christian unions and unemployment? What is a calling, and do all Christians have one – or just those engaged in 'full-time' Christian work? Is ambition legitimate for a Christian, or is it a secular idea? How can we judge, before it is too late, whether our ambition is creative or corrosive? How do we avoid the seduction of wealth that many acquire in abundance in Western economies? What issues arise for a Christian in the City, the media, defence, social work, voluntary work, manual work, teaching, medicine, marketing, pastoral ministry, production, personnel, publishing or tourism? How do we develop a full biblical consideration of themes such as justice, authority and service at work? If the Bible has nothing to say on these issues, it has nothing to say about life.

However, I have not set out to write an encyclopaedia. This is a short, selective book, written by a layman amidst a busy working life with all the normal pleasures and pressures of parenting and family commitments. It may not impress the theological purist, but I hope it will not repel him or her either. It is individual, perhaps even idiosyncratic. I have tried to assemble materials here that anyone and everyone should find useful for constructing their own raft. If I have sometimes 'talked louder than I have walked', perhaps I have done so to keep my spirits up as I make my own journey through the rocky rapids and contend with potentially calamitous capsizes. May each one of us approach our work in the spirit of this exhortation from Paul, the tentmaker:

> Whatever you do, work at it with all your heart, as working for the Lord, not for men... *Colossians 3:23*

Chapter 1

CREATIVITY

Working with wonder: the Creator's design

THE CREATOR'S FIRST ACT

The lights go down, the audience falls silent. The Play is about to begin. As the curtain goes up on the drama of history, we see the main character take centre stage. As he proceeds with the first act, his immense creativity and artistry are immediately evident. It soon becomes clear, too, that he is also the Play's director and producer, and owner of the whole theatre.

Much of the early chapters of Genesis are like the lights panning across a set, revealing God's awesome work in his universe. In the beginning, before the fall, God is working. The environment in which he works is characterised by formlessness, emptiness, and darkness (Gen 1:1,2), but as he progresses with his project:

- formlessness is given shape and proportion;

- emptiness is replaced with fullness and purpose;

- darkness is shot through with light.

God's unmistakable intention is to give order, purpose and meaning wherever chaos would otherwise prevail. Most of us would recognise in this description the way in which human work can be regarded as akin to God's. The shopkeeper, scientist, student, manager, foreman, housewife, fitter, reporter, gardener or doctor can all sense the similarity of their tasks when viewed in this light. Each of us works in cooperation with God to bring order and meaning to our sphere of influence. Without our continuing efforts, chaos would ensue, adversely affecting those who depend on the reliability of our work.

As God begins the work of creation, the Spirit of God hovers like an eagle over its young, ready to catch them should they tumble out of the nest (Gen 1:2; Deut 32:11). The Spirit is demonstrating the supportive concern of one sharing in the demands of the task at hand. The support of the Spirit in our work is no sanctified sentimentality: he is the one who makes the difference between discouragement and perseverance, alienation and fulfilment, inadequacy and excellence. Like the attentive eagle, he helps us to pray faithfully about the demands and dilemmas we face, to think biblically, to work skilfully and to judge soundly.

When Moses set about the task of constructing the sanctuary, he appointed Oholiab and Bezalel to oversee the work of the craftsmen, designers, embroiderers and weavers (Exod 35:30 – 36:1). To undertake this project, God chose the managers and filled them with the Spirit. When the early church went through a burgeoning growth in membership, the church leaders decided to delegate the responsibility of administering the daily distribution of food to the widows of the community, so that they could focus on their core business of prayer and disseminating the word of God. They saw it as essential that the people they chose were 'full of the Spirit and wisdom' (Acts 6:3). So, whether work appears to our eye 'sacred' or 'secular', we too should seek the Spirit's presence and full participation in all that we do.

As Genesis progresses, we see God working to create light and darkness, sky, sea and fertile land, stars and planets, and creatures of water, air and land, including human beings. In all this, there is beauty, profusion, life, colour, contrast, variety and richness. Everything is good and pleasing. However, as the Play continues, we soon discern the tension and disharmony that lurk just below the surface of the action. Let us take a moment to explore some popular notions about why Christians work, and then see if we can arrive at a tentative definition of work from a biblical perspective.

There are three common views about why Christians should work in secular occupations, and you will pick them up in any superficial chat about work. They relate to motive, opportunity and context:

- Christians should work to provide for themselves and their own: 'If a man will not work, he shall not eat' (2 Thess 3:10). Our bodies require fuel to carry out our wider calling as believers, and we should try to avoid becoming an unnecessary burden on others. Our motive for work is money for survival.

- Christians should work in the secular world because of the wonderful opportunities it affords for witness. 'Isn't it lovely', says a beaming friend, 'to have Christians in such and such a position to share the gospel with colleagues.' When we work, we should seize the opportunity for evangelism.

- Christians work because of the fall and Adam's curse (Gen 3:17–19). We live in a world justly condemned by God, and part of his just punishment is that we must sweat among thorns. It is hopeless to indulge in grand ideas about work in such a world – we should just grit our teeth and get on with it. The context in which we work is the fall.

Money, evangelism and the curse: these justifications for work are widely held by Christians, and some may seek to defend them from Scripture. But they will only lead us up a cul-de-sac, because they seek to define work by referring to factors that are outside of work itself. I would like to suggest a different motive, a different opportunity and a different context for work, all of which justify work in its own right. They are all rooted in God himself.

Christians accept without difficulty that God is the Redeemer of humankind. Jesus came to seek and to save the lost, and we acknowledge that as his followers we should obey his will and imitate his example in prayer, Bible study, evangelism, fellowship and serving the needs of those around us. It is in doing these things that we and the Spirit draw people to know Christ and to live for him. However, God is also our Creator, and exactly the same principles – of obeying his will and imitating his example – should under-pin our approach to life in his creation. So, we should work because:

- God created us and put us 'in the Garden of Eden to work it and take care of it' (Gen 2:15). Our motive is to obey his will. While this includes his will that we provide for our needs and the needs of others, it is also his will that we are good stewards of the creation we inhabit.

- God works, and human beings are made in his image. We are given the opportunity to reflect him and become more like him. While this includes bearing witness to his saving grace, it is also about reflecting his qualities as Creator and Redeemer in every part of our lives, including our life at work.

- God delights to share in and support our creative cooperation with him in bringing order and meaning to his universe. Our context may be the fallout of the fall, but we should still seek to collaborate with his original design and to find ways to bring his kingdom into the world.

The common reasons for working described earlier – money, evangelism and the fall – are a recipe for guilt and despair to those who are conscientious about putting them into practice, and for hypocrisy and irrelevance to those who are not. But to obey God's will, reflect his image and collaborate with his design are to establish the foundation for work upon God himself. He is a sturdy enough platform on which to undertake the fulfilling and challenging endeavour that takes up 90,000 hours of our lives.

We will now attempt a biblical definition of work, that it is *the daily exertion, paid or unpaid, in contrast to rest and leisure, which is consistent with God's will, image and design.* By this definition, who works the longest hours and how much they are paid becomes irrelevant: managing a household or voluntary work in the community are accorded as much worth and dignity as the highest paid executive appointment. Our society's tendency to overvalue some careers at the expense of others often leads to our judging people purely in terms of their salary and status. This inflates the proud, diminishes the un(der)paid, and undermines the importance of social relationships among family, friends and communities. The biblical definition given above tries to restore the balance.

In defining what work is, we must also be clear about what it is not. We cannot overlook the fact that while God can create something out of nothing, humankind can only make something out of something. A proper understanding of work fixes the distinction between God and us, but does not detract from the fact that we have much to learn from his work of creating and sustaining the universe. Indeed, it is at this point that nature (which God created) meets culture (which human beings have made) – where God's humble, gracious cooperation with us brings shape, proportion, fullness and light; where we learn from God, imitate him and cooperate with him in bringing order and meaning to his world.

As the first act of the Play draws to a close, we await eagerly the rest of the performance. The main character has captivated us: we want to continue to observe his inimitable work; we want to explore his matchless qualities. It is breathtaking to discover that we are created in his image for a life of purposeful creativity. We will now try to understand that image more fully.

THE CREATOR'S WORK

God's work involves creating and sustaining the universe and everything in it. He creates and sustains:

- every activity under heaven;
- matter in abundance;
- beauty on a lavish scale.

Every activity under heaven

Every legitimate activity under heaven is important to God, but much of it is greatly undervalued by Christians because of the unbiblical, polluting divide we have set up between the secular and the sacred, between ordinary work and work that we consider somehow more 'worthy'.

It often seems to me that, in some Christian circles, the conversation is viewed as far more 'sanctified' if it revolves around prayer and fasting than sexual satisfaction in marriage or fine ale in the pub. But is this right? Is prayer more commendable than a pint, privation more holy than pleasure? How would you rate, in terms of their spiritual value, food, Bible study, architecture, evangelism, technology and fellowship? If I organised two discussion groups at a Christian house party, one on prayer and fasting, and the other on sex and the pint, where would the 'spiritually minded' go? I guess the only response to that is, 'It all depends,' and this would not be to dodge the issue. In certain circumstances, however, the pint and pleasure would indeed be more important than prayer and privation.

Here is what Jesus had to say about prayer:

> 'And when you pray, do not be like the hypocrites, for they love to pray standing in the synagogues and on the street corners to be seen by men ... do not keep on babbling like pagans, for they think they will be heard because of their many words.' *Matthew 6:5,7*

...and about fasting:

> 'When you fast, do not look sombre as the hypocrites do, for they disfigure their faces to show men they are fasting. I tell you the truth, they have received their reward in full.'
>
> *Matthew 6:16*

...and about the pint:

> 'The Son of Man came eating and drinking, and they say, "Here is a glutton and a drunkard..."' *Matthew 11:19*

And this is the apostle Paul, on marital sex:

> Do not deprive each other except by mutual consent and for a time, so that you may devote yourselves to prayer. Then come together again... *1 Corinthians 7:5*

So it may, in some circumstances, be quite justifiable for a couple to miss the church prayer meeting for an evening of marital love. It is a devilish trick to inflate the dangers of the flesh so as to lure us into spiritual errors such as pride, hypocrisy and malice. If we lose the battle against the false divide between the sacred and secular, we lose track of the value of secular work as a worthy occupation. We must, therefore, continually insist that the only true biblical divide is between sin and righteousness.

Let us now address the false idea that jobs can be ranked according to certain criteria, with highest value usually given to those with brains, strength and wealth. In a religious context, a job's status will often depend upon the degree to which it is viewed as 'holy' or 'caring'. Here are some jobs ranked in a fairly typical 'religious' hierarchy:

1 archbishop

2 missionary

3 vicar

4 consultant paediatrician

5 teacher

6 businessman

7 manual technician

It seems to me that 'working worthily' should be more our goal than to do 'worthy work'. Different jobs cannot be ranked, because *all* legitimate work shares in the value of being designed by God for the strengthening, encouragement and comfort of humankind. From God's perspective, the office of archbishop may not be one iota more worthy or more spiritual than that of a shoemaker; yet many Christians seem to struggle with such a proposition.

Entering the ordained ministry, or taking up mission or any other kind of Christian work, may indeed be an admirable mark of obedience; but it can also be marks of ambition and self-will. King Uzziah was castigated and made leprous for taking upon himself the priestly function to which God had not called him (2 Chron 26:16–21). Would it be right to neglect the many kinds of work there are in the world and to concentrate on only the few? What kind of an orchestra would it be if the instrumentalists all decided they wanted to be the conductor or first violinist, and regarded the other, 'lesser' instruments with disdain? A better approach would be to set aside notions of 'higher gifts' and 'worthy work' altogether, and to base our view of a job or activity on whether or not God has called a person to it. If he has, then that job, in his eyes, is as fully equal in value and status as any other. As sixteenth-century Protestant reformer, John Calvin, wrote:

> In everything the call of the Lord is the foundation and beginning of right action. He who does not act with reference to it will never, in the discharge of duty, keep the right path. He will sometimes be able perhaps to give the semblance of something laudable, but whatever it may be in the sight of man, it will be rejected before the throne of God.

Of course, this is not very comforting news for those who are accustomed to all sorts of obsequious privileges based on their assumed status, whose letters are answered more promptly, whose views are sought even on matters they do not understand. Contrast their attitude with that of King David (1 Sam 30): returning from three days on manoeuvres, he and his men arrived home to be greeted with the disastrous news that an Amalekite raiding party had destroyed their town and captured their wives and children. They set off immediately in pursuit, to intercept the enemy and recover their families. However, when they came to a ravine, one-third of his men were unable to cross it because of exhaustion, and they were forced to remain behind with the supplies while the rest pressed on.

Eventually David and his men found the Amalekites, attacked and defeated them, recovering the captives. However, when it came to dividing the spoils of war, troublemakers tried to distinguish between the men who had done the fighting and the 'camp followers' who had looked after the supplies at the ravine: they argued that only those at the front-line should share the plunder. But David rejected this idea outright, even to the extent of enacting legislation to prevent it rearing its divisive head again (vs 23–25).

Equality of worth in employment is unlikely to be popular in the boardroom, but support for this view is strong among the saints. Here are what some powerful advocates of the legitimacy of all kinds of callings have to say:

> There is difference betwixt washing of dishes and preaching of the word of God; but as touching to please God, none at all. *William Tyndale*

> In following your proper calling, no work will be so mean and sordid as not to have a splendour and value in the eye of God. *John Calvin*

> It looks like a small thing when a maid cooks and cleans and does other housework. But because God's command is there, even such a small work must be praised as a service of God. *Martin Luther*

> One thing you should very definitely have in mind – that is that a ministry such as teaching the Bible in a college is no higher a calling intrinsically than being a businessman or doing something else. No one calling is intrinsically higher than another. *Francis Schaeffer*

The work of a Beethoven and the work of a charwoman become spiritual on precisely the same conditions, that of being offered to God, of being done humbly 'as to the Lord'.
C S Lewis

Unfortunately, jobs to which society accords high status bring with them great rewards, which in turn widens social divisions and the gap between rich and poor. When one hears of the payments given to top executives in certain industries in contrast to their support staff, one sees huge, often shocking, disparities. While it may be right to pay those in positions of responsibility more than those who are not, businesses need to design remuneration policies that are suited to their environments and which have a 'felt fairness' within the organisation as a whole. Otherwise, over time, the outcome will be festering resentment and the building up of egos rather than teams.

It is very nearly impossible to relate meaningfully to others without having some idea of what they do at work, whether paid or unpaid. Knowing this opens up all sorts of insights into people's gifts and interests, to say nothing of our common experiences. It is therefore vital that we relate to others without allowing our view of them to be distorted by these false ideas of job status and religious hierarchies. The Bible repeatedly refers to people by their work, often because this gives in shorthand a rough guide to where they are positioned to carry out God's calling on their lives. We meet Alexander the metalworker, Zenas the lawyer, Erastus the director of public works, and Lydia the cloth dealer, to name but a few (Acts 16:11–16; Rom 16:23; 2 Tim 4:14; Titus 3:13). With all of them, their work had a bearing on where and how they carried out the ministry of furthering the gospel.

In fact God's calling adorns and elevates a person's occupation and circumstances far above the dismal preoccupations of human values. Shiphrah and Puah, the Egyptian midwives, were in a key position to defy Pharaoh's male infanticide policy (Exod 1:15–21). As a result, they probably saved Moses' life and thus brought about a change in the course of history which had enormous repercussions for both Egypt and Israel – all because, in their work, they 'feared God' (v 17). In Ephesus, the city clerk used his skills of negotiation and people management to dampen a commotion that could have led to the lynching of Paul and his companions (Acts 19:35–41).

Today, Christians in secular work may be called upon to deal with similar situations and dilemmas that require all the spiritual reserves their faith can muster. They may have to make complex ethical and moral decisions, sometimes with no clear 'right answer'. For example, faced with destitute people living off a nearby rubbish dump, what does a Christian businessman in the Philippines do? Does he give up everything and go to live on the dump with them to preach the good news of Jesus? Does he continue his business, but visit certain groups on the dump to learn what commercial skills they need to build their own livelihood, and then offer them training? Does he work harder to make more money so that he can increase his giving to the needy? These questions cannot be answered without regard to the integrity, interests and circumstances of that businessman. He will certainly need a full assurance of faith and a solid understanding of God's call on his life, as much as any missionary or pastor, to make a good decision on the several legitimate options available.

The debate about the value of 'secular' work has been around for many generations. Cicero wrote, 'The toil of the hired worker who is paid only for his toil and not his artistic skill is unworthy of a freeman and is sordid.' A Jewish Talmudic prayer says, 'I am early to work on the words of the Torah (Law) and they are early to work on the things of no moment.' In the Middle Ages it was common to view the work of the monastery as sacred and secular work as second-best. It seems that the descendants of such views are still with us today. One has only to listen to personal testimonies asserting that God has called an individual to leave secular work, to devote herself to 'God's work', and thereby to enjoy the fulfilment that comes from investing in eternity – 'Now my life really counts!'

That there are a variety of worthwhile activities was obvious to the psalmist in his agrarian society, where raising cattle, growing food, producing wine, making oil and bread were seen not as some reductionists see them today, merely providing fuel for the body, but as given by God to nourish the very heart of humankind (Ps 104:14,15).

Matter in abundance

If God was as uncertain about the value of the material world as some Christians appear to be, he did a very poor job in containing the potential damage! Genesis 1 and 2 are replete with references to expanse, vastness, teeming multitudes, fruitfulness, profusion, increase and plenty. Again, Psalm 104 brilliantly depicts God's passion for matter and his playful delight in his creation ('leviathan, which you formed to frolic there', verse 26), and echoes his preoccupation with creating and sustaining:

> How many are your works, O LORD!
> > In wisdom you made them all;
> > the earth is full of your creatures...
> These all look to you
> > to give them their food at the proper time...
> When you send your Spirit,
> > they are created,
> > and you renew the face of the earth.   *Psalm 104:24,27,30*

Speak to an astronomer about the dimensions of light and matter in the galaxies, or visit a planetarium, and you will struggle to comprehend the prodigious superabundance of our universe. We can observe stars whose light has been travelling at 300,000 kilometres per second for 60 billion years. The edge of the known universe is more than 100 billion trillion kilometres away. For all we know, this edge and all the intervening billions of galaxies may make up only two per cent of the total that we have yet to discover beyond! Question a microbiologist on what he could expect to find in a clod of earth, and a similar volcano of statistics will erupt.

All this is evidence of the Creator's inventiveness. Years of watching the *Discovery* channels and David Attenborough have only increased my awe and wonder at the world around me, which God has made to enthral both him and us. His virtuosity and exuberance are unparalleled. His wisdom is the fountainhead of this array of creativity and matter (Prov 8:22–31): wisdom that later receives its fullest expression in Christ.

And this is no fickle fad prior to the fall. On the contrary, when God visited his creation and undertook the task of redemption, he came as a baby, dependent for food on the breast of his young mother. He took up employment as a labourer for most of his adult life. His resurrection brought him through death to inhabit a body fit for eternity, which could be touched, which bore the marks of the crucifixion, which had flesh and bones, and which enjoyed eating broiled fish (Luke 24:42–43). This new body is recognisably human and prefigures the body that all his people will inhabit for all eternity. And when God required us to enact a suitable remembrance of his Son's death on the cross, he gives us not a slogan nor an idea, but matter – bread and wine.

God became matter, human flesh, yet he was not demeaned by it; rather, through it he transformed humanity. Surely we can bring this reckless generosity and glad profitability of God's creation into our work. Well or even averagely run businesses may know something of this abundance. Sometimes the profits declared by companies are decried as excessive, but no doubt there are situations where such profits are as acceptable as they are unavoidable, if they are put to responsible and generous use (1 Tim 6:17). Of course, there is an obvious difference between making a sound profit and profiteering.

I once visited the public conveniences in Mumbles in Swansea Bay. Outside was a rosette for the best loo in Britain, alongside a fresh basket of flowers packed with colour. Inside smelled pleasant and was spotlessly clean. At eye level where men habitually stand, were information sheets about the weather, tidal times and leisure activities. Here was a team that had turned something so matter of fact into something exceptional.

Beauty on a lavish scale

The multivarious species of trees populating the Garden of Eden were not merely good for food: they were also 'pleasing to the eye' (Gen 2:9). What possible justification can there be for investing so much time and effort in the exquisite design and production of an item that may have a lifespan of only minutes? 'See how the lilies of the field grow ... I tell you that not even Solomon in all his splendour was dressed like one of these' (Matt 6:28,29).

Beauty can easily be associated with decadence, yet it was important for the dignity of the priestly garments that they should be beautiful (Exod 28). Zion is described as 'perfect in beauty' (Ps 50:2). It is because of their beauty that 'the heavens declare the glory of God' (Ps 19:1). Who can contemplate the skies lit up by rich reds, yellows and blues, and not hear 'the work of his hands'? Beauty is a chord in

God's vocal range. Seldom has delight at the excellence of God's work in his creation been voiced more poetically than in Proverbs, where wisdom personified rejoices in God's presence and his creation:

> [When God] marked out the foundations of the earth.
>   Then I was the craftsman at his side.
> I was filled with delight day after day,
>   rejoicing always in his presence,
> rejoicing in his whole world
>   and delighting in mankind.

Proverbs 8:29–31

Truly this is a foretaste of eternity. The Creator is delighted by his work and is apologetic for none of it. His world and our presence in it, cooperating with him, are emphatically affirmed. Beauty is a feature of God's creation that we could strive harder to bring to our work. The architect with a million-pound contract, trying to squeeze more and more profit out of the price – what hope has beauty? The bored clerical assistant drafting a new benefits claims form – what chance to employ a style that is reader-friendly and pleasing to the eye? If, in the Creator's work, function never quenches beauty, nor should it in the work of those created in his image.

Businesses could concern themselves more with aesthetics – in their products, in their operations, in their reception arrangements, for the good of the business and the good of the community. It doesn't even have to be left to managers: even the individual shop assistant has scope to demonstrate creativity and imagination, arranging merchandise so that they display colour and texture, and changing them to reflect the seasons and excite the shopper's eye. 'Beauty is always related to meaning and sense' (H R Rookmaaker). If our work is to have meaning and sense, we will have to consider explicitly how it relates to beauty.

THE CREATOR'S QUALITIES

There are five moral qualities we can ascribe to the Creator, which are evident from the outset of scripture: that he is rational, righteous, responsible, restful and relational. We will look at each of these qualities in turn and see what principles we can glean from them which are relevant to our work. Even though, inevitably, I am writing out of my own experience, it should still be possible for all Christians to apply these principles to whatever work God has placed them in.

Rational

First, God is rational. The central thrust of his activity is to bring order and meaning to his creation and thereby to sustain it. His strategy is evocative of the rational debate that he prefers ('Come now, let us reason together', Isa 1:18): each day he takes a step back to review his work, monitor progress and satisfy himself that his standards have been met, in preparation for the next day (Gen 1:10,12,18,21,25,31).

We too should aspire to be rational in our work: to identify purposeful priorities and stick to them, to help set up systems that ensure the involvement of colleagues in matters that affect them, to share knowledge, to carry out negotiations in a fair and responsible manner. For many people, it is rare to find rational approaches and systems in the workplace, which may often seem to be governed more by competition and self-seeking than openness and working together as a team. I'm sure that most of us want to be regarded as reasonable and measured in our work, to have our ideas sought, debated and valued. Encouraging an atmosphere of competition may motivate a workforce, but so can an environment of rational cooperation. To be rational is to be wise and responsive, not subtle and clever.

Righteous

Second, God is righteous. He gives prominence to 'whatever is true, whatever is noble, whatever is right, whatever is pure, whatever is lovely, whatever is admirable' (Phil 4:8). As he works on his creation, he commends what deserves to be described as 'good' or 'very good'. The seventh day he sets aside as a holy day for rest, blessing and refreshment (Isa 56:2). His pleasure in what is clean and good is palpable.

> For the eyes of the Lord range throughout the earth to strengthen those whose hearts are fully committed to him.
> 2 Chronicles 16:9

> He who walks righteously
>   and speaks what is right,
> who rejects gain from extortion
>   and keeps his hand from accepting bribes,
> who stops his ear against plots of murder
>   and shuts his eyes against contemplating evil –
> this is the man who will dwell on the heights...
>
> Isaiah 33:15,16

Many boardrooms, sales departments and office socials would grind to a halt if such policies as Isaiah is describing were implemented! Yet all who want to live close to God must share his quality of righteousness: 'Lord, who may dwell in your sanctuary? ... He whose walk is blameless and who does what is righteous' (Psalm 15:1–2).

Integrity is often talked about at work – most businesses make much of their commitment to integrity, recognising that it plays an indispensable part in their capacity to survive. I have in front of me a copy of a 'Policy on Business Ethics' from one of the world's largest multinationals. All employees have to sign it. It states, 'The policy of this company continues to be one of strict observance of all laws applicable to its business. Even where the law is permissive, the company chooses the course of the highest integrity.'

There is little doubt that this is the attitude we would like to project, but, in the practical pressures of doing business, the reality may be somewhat different. Some of the most reputable names in the world get swallowed up in moral disaster. To be sure, some businesses would not see it this way, those where the only criterion for proceeding with an advantageous proposal would be 'Is it legal? Is it auditable? Will I get caught?' Subsequent shipwreck is described as 'bad luck', not 'shocking judgement'. An example might be the provision of pornographic channels in an otherwise respectable hotel chain that preys on the lonely business traveller. Choice and competition would view this as a good investment, yet righteousness would reject it as a stain on that company's integrity and conscience.

The decline of righteousness in the workplace should not be underestimated. A generation ago, people would leave their offices or desk drawers unlocked. Today you often need a swipe card or to know a code to get into reception. Introducing myself to a new colleague at a board meeting, I was affably offered illegal air tickets purchased in soft currency from a holiday destination at a substantial discount. This was seen as a kind gesture towards my vacation. A neighbour talks of acquiring goods for me without putting them through his company books. Tradesmen submit two estimates without stopping to check whether I might be a VAT inspector.

Even worse is the colleague who claims to have thought up every idea, blames others for her own shortcomings, whose words are sometimes accurate but never quite truthful. There are those who seek to entice you into gossip, backbiting or office politics. The development of whistle-blowing procedures is an attempt to redress the balance in situations where power is abused by those senior enough to feel immune from accountability. All these examples show the power of unethical activity and the urgent need for ethical integrity.

Long-service awards for loyalty, performance-related pay and bonuses are familiar methods of commending staff and affirming what is right. *The One Minute Manager*, a world best-seller, is designed in three easy steps to increase productivity, profits and prosperity. What is described as the 'second secret' are 'One Minute Praisings' which involve praising people on the spot, stopping for a moment to let them feel how good you feel, and shaking hands in a way that makes it clear that you support their success in the organisation. Of course, such behaviour without a moral and righteous base could be viewed as little more than insincere and manipulative, but if it truly reflects endorsement for righteousness it accords with the image of God. Indeed, one of the signs of government is to praise those who do right (1 Pet 2:14).

Why not spend a few moments now asking yourself how many times this past week you have stopped to thank, praise or endorse someone who has done right, perhaps at some considerable expense of time or effort. More than once in my experience as a manager I have become aware of a rapid decline in a person's performance, and mounting negativity and criticism. Usually I have found that it is because they have gained the impression that their work is not valued. Even when the reality is entirely the opposite, my failure to give positive affirmation has been the direct cause of disheartening a colleague. Clearing the air as early as possible can produce a dramatic change overnight! Such is the power of acknowledging what is right and good.

Responsible

When God created us, he provided for us (Gen 1:29). Whatever freedoms he gives us to develop and enjoy his creation, we are expected to take care of both it and ourselves (Gen 2:15). It was never intended that we should impoverish our own generation or mortgage the choices of future generations by plundering the earth's resources and giving nothing back. God is committed to the sustainable development of his created order, and his ideas of stewardship are indispensable and relevant to current debates on sustainability.

Many corporations these days are apparently committed to conservation and green issues – having such a reputation, they feel, will give them a competitive edge in recruitment and marketing. In their internal and external policies, organisations stress their desire to be known as caring and responsible, willing to shoulder the burden rather than shirk difficult decisions. Many local councils are taking up the challenge and designing sustainable policies for their communities. Consumers too seem willing to pay higher prices for organic and environmentally friendly products, to boycott GM foods and to support fair trade. Governments give earnest consideration to setting up well-run public transport systems and getting people out of their cars and onto the train. How far people are really willing to go on this issue is still an open question. To create proper sustainable development will require wholesale changes in lifestyle, meaning that those living in wealthy developed countries will have to make a dramatic reductions in the consumption of products and in our standard of living if the earth's ecosystems are not to be damaged beyond repair.

The Creator exercises dominion over the entire environment, animate and inanimate, and this dominion he has delegated uniquely to humankind:

Then God said, 'Let us make man in our image, in our like-
ness, and let them rule over the fish of the sea and the birds of
the air, over the livestock over all the earth and over all the
creatures that move along the ground.

So God created man

in his own image…

God blessed them and said to them, 'Be fruitful and increase
in number, fill the earth and subdue it.

Genesis 1:26–28

Those hostile to the Christian tradition often see in the
command to 'fill the earth and subdue it' the source of all
that has gone wrong with the relationship between human
beings and their planet. In their view, unrestrained population explosion underpinned by the hostility shown by some
religious quarters to birth control, and the excessive deple-
tion of limited natural resources, are all a direct consequence
of the religious view of humanity's right of dominion.

There is a counter-response to this accusation, which
there is not time to go into here; however, it is worth stating
what every manager knows – delegating responsibility does
not mean abdicating responsibility. The concept of responsibility combines the notion of 'caring for' something with
that of 'ruling over' it, as the phrase 'to take responsibility'
implies. When God commissioned us to take care of the
earth, he did not mean take care of it any way we like.
Creation belongs to him, he remains in charge (Ps 24:1), and
he wishes us to carry out our governing role in accordance
with *his* desires for creation.

For example, I may have been delegated the freedom to
manage in my job, but this comes with the proviso that I act
in accordance with my boss's policies: I have no freedom to
plough my own furrow in any direction that suits me.
Likewise, human beings may be delegated the freedom to

rule over their environment, but that comes with the proviso that our rule is consistent with God's purpose (his policy) for creation. And since God's purpose is to preserve creation's good, then we should make that good our aim also. God's mandate to 'fill the earth and subdue it' is, therefore, a mandate to demonstrate caring responsibility. That mandate does not undermine his ownership: on the contrary, it underlines it.

Sustainable development will only flourish when it is given more than lip service, when it has breadth and depth, when it is openly declared in our corporate value statements, when we make it an essential ingredient of the spiritual, economic, social, cultural and environmental dimensions of human life. Human beings have demonstrated that we are capable of 'creative dominion' as we advance in the fields of agriculture, art, botany, poetry, chemistry, literature, medicine, drama, industry, music and technology. By all these means we have 'subdued' the earth and brought huge benefits to the human race. However, we have also shown our propensity to destroy human life, exploit or decimate other species for profit, and pollute and destroy the earth we inhabit.

In these and other ways, we human beings, made in God's image, fail in our delegated authority to rule responsibly and exercise dominion over our world in a way that accords with our Creator's intentions. He was willing to take risk. We have all experienced the manager who delegates a task and then interferes at every turn, allowing the other no hope of ownership, personal achievement or dignity. But when God entrusted us with his creation, he did so in a way that preserved our dignity and gave us the freedom to choose (with some limits, Gen 2:16,17). He allowed Adam to name the beasts and the birds as he wished (Gen 2:19,20), to call them 'aardvark' or 'great crested grebe' (or the Hebrew equivalent) and, if this was not elegant enough, he offered the alternatives of *orycterops afer* and *podiceps cristatus*: 'whatever the man called each living creature, that was its name.'

Restful

God is restful – that is, rhythm and rest accompany all his activities. We will see later, in more detail, the dangers that arise from disregarding the Creator's image in this respect when we look at stress. Let us just note here how the rhythmic refrain, 'and there was evening, and there was morning', is repeated throughout the creation account (Gen 1:5,8,13,19, 23,31). The climax of rest and blessing on the seventh day introduces a hint of celebration. So important is this rhythm in establishing a balanced and healthy lifestyle that God subsequently enshrines the principle in a formal commandment (Exod 20:8–11).

In the West, long hours are an integral part of working life. A front-page headline in *The Times* reports: 'Ambitious lawyers for influential law firms in Washington routinely work 12-hour days, seven days a week, as they aim for the top.' In biblical thinking, the driven achiever catapulting up the corporate pay scales is not so much astonishing as pitiable. I once went door-to-door visiting, and was invited in to talk by a man in his fifties. He had been a senior executive in an international firm, and had spent the past twenty years jetting around the world week by week, staying in 5-star hotels. As a result, his health was shattered, and the company doctors had insisted on premature retirement. This man had no financial worries – but then no amount of money would buy back his health. What would the next twenty years propped up in a 5-star armchair feel like?

Nevertheless, Scripture is solidly behind hard work and the self-starter, and castigates laziness:

> Go to the ant, you sluggard;
>> consider its ways and be wise!
> It has no commander,
>> no overseer or ruler,
> yet it stores its provisions in summer
>> and gathers its food at harvest.   *Proverbs 6:6,7*

But 'Meditation as well as work, contemplation as well as action, being as well as doing, companionship with God as well as serving God, are the creative mandates of man' (James Houston). The Christian life should show abundant evidence of rhythm and rest, exertion and leisure, high performance given and holiday leave taken. We will explore this further in the next chapter.

Relational

God is relational. He values the relationship he has with us, his creation, and gives pre-eminence to human beings, distinguishing between the creation which is 'good' and humankind in his image, whom he describes as 'very good'. Indeed, God himself *is* relationship – Father, Son and Holy Spirit. He offers humankind his friendship, but he also anticipates the importance of equal companionship and responds to it with breathtaking imagination – marriage (Gen 2:18–24). Indeed, God's desire for close relationship with us is such that 'in love he predestined us to be adopted as his sons through Jesus Christ' (Eph 1:5).

Any analysis of contemporary Western society reveals a startling divergence at this point between the biblical mind and the natural mind (1 Cor 2:10–16). The low priority given in practice to relationships is profoundly depressing. Largely, this low view may be accidental, as other agenda and priorities preoccupy and distract us. For example, a light-hearted look at a marriage in a rut, the film *Shirley Valentine*, struck a chord for many with its sympathetic portrayal of a woman worn down and disheartened by being the only member of her family interested in relationships. But it is noticeable how many relationships in the story are seen from Shirley's point of view as negative, worthless and ripe for escaping.

Shirley is not malicious in this: she is pursuing the goal of self-worth and personal freedom. In the process we find her at odds with her school chums, even the brightest of whom we encounter later as a high–class call-girl. Her head teacher is a silly twit, her neighbour is a nosy snob, her children are lazy louts, her holiday companion is a selfish madam, her hotel waiter (Tom Conteh) is a lying philanderer, and her husband is a crushing bore. No wonder Shirley opts out of relationships with all their demands and pressures, and embraces a brief holiday in the sun, a small adultery on a pleasure boat, and an evening routine of solitary sundowners looking out over glorious sunsets. So much more satisfying than struggling with real relationships. But in crossing the line of betrayal and adultery, and justifying this shock tactic as a possible freshener for her marriage, she puts self-fulfil-ment above faithful relationships.

Sexual relationships in contemporary films are often depicted as the first contact made between strangers, with the focus on animal appetite, sexual technique, silent indif-ference and joyless pleasure. When Marlon Brando's lover in *Last Tango in Paris* asks his name, he cries, 'We don't want any names here.' In Stanley Kubrick's last film, *Eyes Wide Shut*, the on-screen marriage of Tom Cruise and Nicole Kidman is stretched to breaking point by their fantasies of sexual intimacy outside their relationship. Unusually, they draw back when they recognise that 'a dream is never just a dream' and that a precious relationship can be laid waste even by a straying imagination. Milan Kundera's *The Unbearable Lightness of Being* remains one of the most poignant evocations of the pain of unrelational sex.

These are attempts at depersonalised, decontextualised coupling with limited intimacy, gentleness, commitment or consequences. Recreation without responsibility. Abandonment without accountability. Passion without purity. The rise in office affairs – even discussed in business magazines as the ultimate perk (according to a headline I read some time ago in a management journal) – shows that private values are never very far from public behaviour.

It is worth taking time to consider other examples of this kind of thinking which relate to work, whether they are accidental or deliberate, whether led by conscious policy or driven by unchallenged expediency. The natural mind accords higher value to business rather than family, to career rather than relationships, to material riches rather than the riches of friendship. A person at the top of corporate life is regarded as a dazzling success, to be envied even though in the background there are three broken marriages, a succession of affairs, alienated offspring, a severe drink problem and elderly parents ignored.

Personal career success can be more highly valued than the business that supports everyone else's career. A friend in a City bank said he was becoming disillusioned with the number of graduates who asked about company cars at their first interviews fresh out of university. On learning that they would have to wait two or three years before that happened, a proportion walked away saying they had no intention of staying with any organisation that long. The banker wondered aloud how any business could flourish if there was so little regard paid to loyalty and the company's interests. Of course, the culture of pursuing profit at all costs, which exists in some companies, cultivates such responses from staff. When the acquisition of power, status, worth, health, wealth and self-fulfilment are viewed as deeply important, earning money becomes something that requires an individual's undivided attention at the cost of broader loyalties. But these are shallow goals: 'They rarely sustain people in deep personal crisis and do not carry anyone beyond the threshold of death' (Robert Banks).

Less and less time is invested in relationships. Returning to work after childbirth is often regarded more positively than remaining at home to child care. Dependant relationships (the very old or very young) are largely delegated to others. Professional nannies have been quoted as expressing astonishment at the extent to which some parents are willing to forego the unique intimacy of their children's childhood. Time contributed to the job is measured on a scale of quantity – loyal employees are expected to put in long hours. Time contributed to the family is measured on a scale of quality. But who judges the value of that contribution? In the workplace it is the one who receives it (the boss or customer), but in the home it is the one who gives it (the parent). Imagine reversing these approaches!

Contacts at work are most highly valued when they are useful, and often an exaggerated, false familiarity can grow up. It is rare for relationships at work to be deep and valued in their own right. Do not bank on being remembered at your workplace twenty weeks after retiring – you may be disappointed. Meanwhile, in the community, neighbours say nothing to each other for decades, beyond ritual courtesies. We once engaged a roofing contractor who boasted genially to us that he had not spoken to any of his neighbours since he moved in seven years earlier. He was proud at having killed off any attempt at neighbourliness. In his view, relationships were not worth the aggravation. But if we are relational beings, we should be trying continually to deepen, broaden and strengthen relationships at every opportunity.

Every chief executive and personnel director would love to be able to make people their priority: recruitment literature and annual reports say a lot about making the most of 'our most precious resource'. However, putting this into practice is all too often lost in the 'jungle' of competition, where only the fittest survive, and 'we owe it to all our employees to demand the best and to let the rest go'.

One can only wonder what influence a material change in attitude on this point would have had on the profits, productivity and prosperity of certain companies featured in the news over the years. I attended a senior managers' programme at a leading business school, where we debated the central priority of business, its *raison d'être*. There was an overwhelming consensus that the maximisation of profit and the creation of wealth should lie at the heart of any corporate mission statement. The first duty was to maximise the shareholder's investment, which is measured in terms of the return on investment or on managed assets, or of giving value for money. Do those of you in business agree with that? I do not believe this is a biblical perspective.

An enterprise exists to serve people's needs and to give value in doing so. If we cannot accept that as a major goal of an organisation's *raison d'être*, then the battle is lost before we start. The Papal Encyclical on Work (*Laborem Exercens*) states:

> Work corresponds to the biblical concept only when throughout its performance man manifests himself and proves that he is the one who has dominion. The primacy of man over things must be set at the forefront and emphasised. It is wrong for an economy to be more or less completely guided by the criterion of maximum profitability.

A company does indeed have an obligation to serve the shareholder by creating wealth as a fair return for the investor – I have no quarrel with the concept of profits, even very considerable profits that the proper use of modern management strategies and technologies makes readily attainable in certain fields. But the shareholder is only one such relationship in the working life; there are many others, equally important, and each brings with it important obligations that every organisation needs to work out in detail.

There are the obligations to staff – to give them decent pay and conditions of service, equal opportunities and suitable resources for them to do their work. There are the obligations to provide the information base and professional development opportunities needed to grow the business. To the trade unions, where they exist, there is a duty of respect and cooperation, acknowledging legitimate differences of interest in securing common aims. To the customer, there is a duty of good faith and value for money. To external contractors and suppliers, there are obligations of fair tendering and evaluation procedures, and the prompt settlement of invoices. To the public and community, there are particular social obligations in terms of health-and-safety and stability of employment. To the government, there is the duty to observe legal restrictions and to render to the Revenue all necessary taxation. Many of these obligations do not sit comfortably with the simple maximisation of profit. Nevertheless, profit remains a key test of whether a business is providing a quality service and doing so in a way that offers value for money. But profit alone cannot be allowed to supersede relationships, for that way lies a road littered with broken people.

Some of the more farsighted corporate mission statements I have seen do attempt to give priority to relationships; but most do not and would dismiss them as impractical. But good relationships are crucial to the quality of working life. When a team pulls together in difficult circumstances and pulls off a wonderful win, the energy released can be astounding. There is nothing more invigorating than to work with colleagues who are sensitive, alert to family commitments, loyal and supportive when the chips are down.

Too often, however, work relationships are perfunctory,

impersonal, technocratic, minimalist, treacherous even. 'My' success and 'my' career become higher priorities, self-interest reigns and the achievements of others are denigrated. Many working practices seem to accentuate accountability and blame rather than support. Alliances are deftly cemented by demeaning and flattering colleagues in proportion to their usefulness. Information is manipulated, withheld, leaked, distorted, until a ferment of mistrust finally begins to close down healthy relationships. To disregard the roles of people in the workplace is a serious misjudgement. For Christians, work is primarily a service to humankind in the service of God, and the working arena should be shaped with this in mind.

SUMMARY

God is extravagantly creative. We are created in his image and so our work expresses his creativity. Creativity enlivens everything it touches with deeper order, purpose and meaning. The Creator's work involves creating and sustaining, and in these activities both his world and our work in it are emphatically affirmed. All distinctions between the sacred and secular are irrelevant – only sin and righteousness should be distinguished. Then we will be free to reflect God's image through our work, paid or unpaid. The ultimate endorsement of ordinary activities, physical matter and the beauty of our created environment was God's willingness to be born as a man on earth. He raised Jesus from death in a new and indestructible body that was recognisably human. He celebrates the death of his Son on the cross through the symbols of bread and wine.

The Creator's qualities – the five Rs – are actions and attitudes that reflect his image. This image needs constantly to be realised both in us and in our work. It is arguable that best practice in certain organisations does indeed reflect God's values in being rational, righteous, responsible, restful and relational, and these should always be our attitudes and standards at work. However, organisations and the people in them have their shortcomings in these areas which we as Christians will want to challenge from the inside. Most of all, we need to acknowledge our own shortcomings when we fail to live up to God's standards; when we are quick to judge and condemn others but slow to see it when we let others down.

We need to look more closely at God's character to recover what it means to reflect his image, since we are called to do this in every aspect of our work. We could start by reviewing our attitudes to work in general, as well as our attitudes to our own contribution at work. We should try to see where the five qualities of the Creator that we looked at earlier are already evident, and where they need to become more so. We will want to give particular attention to his relational characteristics. As we do this, we need to bear in mind that our overall aim should be to serve God better.

We should also give thanks that, however mundane our work may seem, God does not call us to 90,000 hours of hard labour. He calls us to cooperate with him by bringing order, purpose and meaning to our small part of his enterprise. In doing so, our individual creativity, skills and interests will find expression alongside those of others. This is an intrinsic part of our calling, contribution and output at work, and should be celebrated as such. If we never lose sight of God's creativity, we will never exhaust the reservoir of inspiration that makes our ordinary work extraordinary, as we seek to live our lives in his image as Creator and Redeemer.

Chapter 2

REST

Spanner in the works: the fall's impact

UNDERSTANDING STRESS

With the fall comes God's curses and punishments for human disobedience (Gen 3) and these, in turn, have a profound impact on human work. They bring about what was not originally a part of work but which is now familiar to every working person – stress. The garden enthusiast becomes the hard-pressed farm labourer. Restful activity gives way to chronic pressure. In the next two chapters, we will explore the gap that has opened up between work as God intended it and work as we experience it. However, before we do, let's take a moment to fill in the context.

Temptation begins with the serpent questioning the word of God: 'Did God really say, "You must not eat from any tree in the garden"?' (Gen 3:1). Eve proves amenable to this line of questioning and slyly exaggerates the rigour of God's command (vs 2,3). Seizing upon her willingness to doubt God, the serpent then flatly contradicts him (vs 4,5). Eve, enticed by the lust of the flesh, the lust of the eyes and the pride of life, disobeys God and eats the forbidden fruit. Adam eagerly becomes her accomplice in disobedience (v 6), for which he is held accountable theologically and federally for the spread of sin and death to all humankind (Rom 5:12–14). Guilt, shame and subterfuge immediately stain their relationship (Gen 3:7) and they both actively seek to avoid God (vs 8–10). Their preoccupation is now to find someone to blame for their sorry state (vs 11–13).

This downward spiral is a familiar enough human experience. Human beings are all too prone to surrendering their convictions and succumbing to avarice and the desire for power. We drag others in to lend respectability to the enterprise ('everyone's doing it, so it must be OK') and then engage in a number of hopeless measures to mask the inevitable degradation. The spiral ends with God's judgement, searing in its exposure of the truth and withering in its severity. Conflict, pain and alienation are the fruit of this rotten seed. This pattern is replicated in our work.

Stress defined

It is important to emphasise that the word 'stress' does not itself appear in the Bible. There are many ideas in Scripture that reflect what we call stress today, but they need to be handled with care if we are not to make unbiblical assumptions. *Stress comes about when spiritual, psychological, emotional and physical pressures mount up which we cannot face without calling on additional resources.*

This is, for me, a broad enough definition that takes account of pressures which may be gradual or sudden, enjoyable or wearisome, external or internal, imposed or self-inflicted.

Sometimes stress is unavoidable: however careful a driver you are, you cannot ensure that another driver will never crash into you. And there will be times when Christians in particular have to endure stress as part of their discipleship – in extreme circumstances, this is what the martyrs went through. But stress need not always be bad; rather, it can be an exhilarating and life-enhancing experience when people are able to draw on adequate resources – from within or without – to help them handle stress creatively. A Formula One driver, for example, would be a hazard both to himself and others if he did not relish the stress of his sport. If he is able to draw on his deepest internal resources, and is supported by intense training and team support, he can endure enormous yet delicious levels of stress in his quest to win the race. However, when an individual does not have the resources to cope, stress becomes overwhelming.

It is not always easy to tell when one has crossed the line between healthy stress that can be endured and the unhealthy stress that is heading towards mental or physical collapse. People's levels of endurance will vary according to their temperament and constitution. While we can learn invaluable lessons – about God, others or ourselves – when we go through times of extreme stress, we need to take action if we are not to suffer serious breakdown. This could range from applying a simple remedy for physical symptoms such as anaemia, to undergoing a complex range of interventions for severe psychological disturbance.

Before we go on, it would be advisable to touch on a common Christian myth about stress. There are those who suggest that the coming of Jesus has swept away all stress: now that he is in their lives, Christians should either not encounter stress at all or they should not feel it. I share neither this view nor this experience. God in his fatherly wisdom has punished all humankind. It is true that a Christian whose life is in Christ has gained the power to overcome death, and here and now will begin to taste the first-fruits of his harvest (1 Cor 15:22,23), but the full harvest is yet to come. In the meantime, God is not some giant paracetamol in the sky! He does not shield Christians from the problems of life.

Has Satan called a truce? Do Christian women going through labour without an epidural yell less? Does a

Christian manager handle pressure on the job without turning a hair? Does a church never encounter conflict? No. The full experience of salvation, although assured and tasted in this life, is 'an inheritance that can never perish, spoil or fade – kept in heaven ... ready to be revealed in the last time' to those who are kept by God's power. This is our 'living hope' (1 Pet 1:3–5), not our daily entitlement. In fact, stress is more of a fundamental reality than we would like to think. It is, as it were, built into the fabric of life since the fall. It should not be treated like some peculiar disease from which 'successful Christians' are immune. Indeed, to view stress as a weakness may be to condemn many sufferers to hiding themselves away with their burdens.

Susceptibility to stress

It is possible, these days, to identify the factors that will help us to predict when stress is likely to occur. The fall has made each and every one of us less whole than we might have been. By nature, therefore, we are all more or less vulnerable to stress, temperamentally, genetically and psychologically. However, research suggests that certain factors make us more prone to stress than others.[1] There may be a limit to what we can do about these, but it is valuable to be aware of them. For example, here are four factors that link personality with stress.

Emotional suppression

This is often associated with traditional toughness, when people are less self-disclosing and undemonstrative by nature. An individual who likes to play it cool, adopt a stiff upper lip and respond to every crisis with outward indifference, will often inwardly be experiencing enormous tension.

Timidity

Dominant personalities and rigid hierarchies can be intimidating and lead to subtle forms of bullying. A fearful disposition unwilling to challenge such cultures will quickly become prey to insecurity and anxieties about self-worth.

Workaholism

The workaholic temperament is characterised by an obsession with work-related activities at the expense of spiritual, social, family and physical priorities. Workaholics may be highly valued in some work cultures because they appear to offer a commitment no one else can match. However, workaholism is in fact a species of immaturity and self-indulgence.

Type A personality

This personality is well-known to psychologists as one that puts itself under pressure in the bid to achieve success and recognition. The Type A individual talks explosively, walks and eats rapidly, waits impatiently and evaluates everything by numbers. Such a person will finish other people's sentences for them, and feels guilty about relaxing. Anything that moves is regarded as competition to be outpaced. As one who has a tendency towards this personality, I sometimes find myself competing in the swimming pool with a complete stranger who is unaware of my existence, merely because he is already half way down the length and moving fast! Type A will only read poetry when on a speed-reading course and he needs to get through all the material.

Susceptibility to stress may also arise out of an individual's lifestyle. Research identifies factors such as the absence of:

- regular, balanced meals;
- adequate sleep patterns;

- exercise to the point of perspiration at least twice a week; and

- access to close friends or family, where frank and personal conversation occurs.

Cigarette smoking, or drinking too much alcohol or coffee, cola or tea each day are also significant.

Sources of stress

There are hundreds of different sources of stress, which we will now separate into three main categories – conflict, pain and alienation. Clearly, the strategies for alleviating stress will be different for each.

Conflict

> So the Lord God said to the serpent, 'Because you have
> done this,
> ...I will put enmity
>   between you and the woman,
>   and between your offspring and hers;
> he will crush your head,
>   and you will strike his heel.
> To the woman he said,
> ...'Your desire will be for your husband,
>   and he will rule over you.'   *Genesis 3:14–16*

Whatever the precise meaning of these verses, it is not in dispute that conflict, manipulation and subjugation are inherent in human relations, all too often engulfing them in injustice and malice. Conflict between people at work comes in all forms. Racism, classism, ageism, tribalism and sexism flourish despite the legislation and education programmes aimed at eradicating them. The Inquiry into the murder of

Stephen Lawrence coined the phrase 'institutional racism' to underline the reality of the unwitting racism that can seep into the culture of organisations. Unwitting it may be, but unjust it still is when it impacts negatively on someone's work prospects.

Conflict is not confined to the 'cut and thrust' world of private enterprise. Sir John Harvey-Jones's troubleshooting took him to the Shropshire District Health Authority, a publicly funded body with, supposedly, none of the stresses of the commercial environment. He was intrigued by the political conflicts he found there:

> I became fascinated by the problems of managing a public authority. I hadn't realised how complex and difficult the problems are. All managers must develop political skills in the broadest sense. But this is nothing to the political skills a health service manager needs to operate. They must develop an extraordinary talent for selling their ideas. Health service managers who can pick their way through this minefield will have developed skills that many private sector managers would envy.

Jokes about conflict with the boss are as popular as those about the mother-in-law. Trade unions form to protect workers from arbitrary autocrats; commissioners are appointed to protect members from their unions. Differences of personality in the workplace give occasion to the drawing up of laborious grievance or collective dispute procedures and disciplinary arrangements to assist as a last resort, before it all goes to an industrial tribunal. People storm out of the workplace claiming constructive dismissal, while others are driven away by malice. If some managers abuse their position to oppress their staff, and deserve punishment, an increasing number of staff see litigation as a quick route to a jackpot. The costs and risks involved in defending even flimsy allegations have spawned a billion pound industry of 'split the difference' settlements, where both sides meet half way in the interests of avoiding bills rather than answering justice. This leads to massive cost to the taxpayer and public services. Industrial espionage, a well-placed computer virus, commercial vandalism and strike action can all decimate a business.

It seems that conflict is ever present in the world of work and may even permeate the home, particularly if the main breadwinner becomes choked with self-importance and disdains the unpaid work in the domestic sphere that earns less kudos in contemporary society.

Pain

> To the woman he said,
> 'I will greatly increase your pains in childbearing;
>   with pain you will give birth to children...'
> To Adam he said, ...
> 'Cursed is the ground because of you;
>   through painful toil you will eat of it
>   all the days of your life.
> It will produce thorns and thistles for you,
>   and you will eat the plants of the field.
> By the sweat of your brow
>   you will eat your food...'   *Genesis 3:16–19*

Hard labour now replaces the easy fertility of Eden. The ground on which we work has been cursed and will never perform quite as we wish. Productive employment is stalked by sweaty labour. Even when we succeed, there are always more mountains to climb, oceans to navigate. Impenetrable peaks and devastating troughs inexplicably beset us, whether we work in farming or the money markets. Success goes to dishonest buffoons, while conscientious talent makes no headway. As so clearly demonstrated in the reality TV show, the 'survivor' is the least threatening, least offensive member of the team who comes out as the winner who takes all.

Working for high rewards may turn out to be chasing a rainbow. If the yield does arrive, it may come too late − ill health and old age rob the prize of its glitter. Racing adrenalin gives way to unrelenting exhaustion. No job or promotion is ever quite as fantastic in practice as it seemed in prospect. Children who might have inherited the wealth generated over years, may subsequently have been lost in bitter custody hearings, or antagonised by years of disagreement; or they may not have actually been born at all, having been decided against earlier at the formative stage of a career. Alternatively, they may be all too obviously waiting in the wings to get their hands on the lucre to support an indolent lifestyle.

For all these and other reasons, mental and physical breakdowns have multiplied. Mysterious malaises such as ME and repetitive strain injury (RSI), along with the poor physical fitness that results from an increasingly sedentary working lifestyle, bring debilitating tiredness and make it harder to deal with increased workloads and long hours. The whole area of ill health, whether a consequence or a cause of stress, brings pain, disappointment and frustration. When our health stumbles, it becomes difficult to enjoy anything in life, including our work.

Alienation

> ...'until you return to the ground,
> since from it you were taken;
> for dust you are
> and to dust you will return.'

> ...And the Lord God said, 'The man has now become like one of us, knowing good and evil. He must not be allowed to reach out his hand and take also from the tree of life and eat, and live for ever.' So the Lord God banished him from

the Garden of Eden to work the ground from which he had been taken. After he drove the man out, he placed on the east side of the Garden of Eden cherubim and a flaming sword flashing back and forth to guard the way to the tree of life. *Genesis 3:19–24*

The echo of Adam and Eve's expulsion remains audible forever, like a single rifle shot continuously echoing round a canyon. Eden was a place of communion and security, innocence, peace, leisure, pleasure and purpose; but human disobedience led to our being driven away from all this. Instead we inhabit a world of hidden and unknown dangers, cut off from the God and Father we rejected. Now we are bedevilled by incessant dreams of what might have been. We can never quite settle for what we have. Life seems absurd and meaningless, and a sense of alienation sets in. This alienation may be expressed as a problem with self-worth or fulfilment. It may be an ill-defined unease that contradicts our outward stability and success. It can stir up a sense of churning, a longing for change and a lack of contentment.

Alienation prevents people from feeling at home with themselves and their environment. It poisons all pleasures. It may strike at the hour when you are most unguarded. It may melt away at night only to be there as you wake the next morning. It foments a persistent question mark: Why am I doing all this? What's the point? Is it worth all the effort? Do I belong here? Is this all I can expect? Why are you downcast, O my soul, and why are you so disturbed within me? Am I the only one to feel like this?

The minimal, mechanical contribution that many people give to their work often contrasts sharply with the breadth and imagination of their contribution and creativity in other enterprises, voluntary or sporting. Boredom and depression at work, and methods of mindless mass production, are all symptoms of alienation which we should rightly rebel against and change. Sometimes, however, people go to the opposite extreme and hide their alienation under a packed schedule, crowding out self-doubt and a sense of futility with busyness. They may be tempted to point up the lushness of their success, dogged by the sinking feeling that in the end it may not mean that much. Others may shore up their sense of worth by denigrating the work of those around them. A 'fast-track civil servant' and a 'public sector bureaucrat' could equally describe the same job. The word 'accountant' may be a term of commendation or abuse. Hence we demean others and promote ourselves in our attempts to lessen the sense of alienation that in reality springs with fangs from our soul.

Most commonly, alienation at work arises from the distorted values prevalent at work. The structures and culture of an organisation are usually a product of its priorities. These may be no less pervasive for being unwritten, even unacknowledged. The presidency of Richard Nixon is a good example. We may never know the whole truth about Watergate, but my own conclusion at the time was that Nixon did not authorise the break-in nor did he know about it. Indeed, I believe he would have stopped it had he known about it. Nevertheless, he was entirely responsible for Watergate, and not just in his capacity as leader.

All the evidence, including Nixon's autobiography, suggests that a culture within his administration had been created where those who wished to succeed knew this could be done by promoting the President. The values that imperceptibly emerged did not require presidential endorsement in every detail, because what was good for Nixon was obviously good for America. In such a culture, Watergate, or something like it, was bound to happen. It was the outcome of a 'must-win' government alienated from its 'must-serve' legitimacy. We have to look deeper than the mission statement of a company to discover the formative priorities at work in an organisation. We may start with its mission statement and see what importance is given to serving people, achieving excellence and offering value. But we know that such statements are usually heavily sanitised for public consumption, and should be weighed against actual practice.

Alienation at work may be deliberately fomented. The Lord God cursed the serpent and put enmity between it and humankind, and now the serpent continually seeks to strike at the Achilles heel of humankind, preying upon our innate weakness and exposing our flaws with humiliating ruthlessness. Temptation comes in many guises, and we find ourselves alienated from our own responses. A senior cabinet minister, happily married with grown-up children and pretensions to prime ministerial office, is caught committing adultery. A successful sporting millionaire with no financial needs is discovered defrauding the Inland Revenue. A world-famous film actress is arrested for shoplifting. A respectable international businessman is reported to be addicted to narcotics. These are hardy perennials that always make it into the headlines of tabloid newspapers and gossip magazines.

And these temptations are not confined to the rich and famous. Look in any workplace and you will find the evidence. The senseless lure of overstated expense accounts that gain a few pounds but which could wreck a career. The excesses of the office party. The petty pilfering of stationery. The deal that requires long journeys when the mileage rate is attractive, but which can be concluded with a quick phone call when it is not. Using company restructuring to settle old scores. Booking the annual conference within easy access to pornographic video stores, brothels and gambling establishments, to ensure a larger turnout. The delicious poison of the coffee-morning gossip, the superciliousness of the gin-and-tonic soirée. The business dinners where every conversation presents an opportunity to boast undetected. The conversations at work about work, which never stray beyond work lest our familiar work uniforms are stripped away. All these further underline our frailty, our being forced to live with failure in an alien environment.

Signs of stress

It is not enough to be aware of our susceptibility to stress and the sources of stress. While such awareness can help us reduce the likelihood of stress, it is equally important that we are alert to the signs of stress so that we can take action to remedy them early.

The signs of stress are fairly obvious and may commonly be observed as follows:

Effect on feelings	Effect on behaviour	Effect on health
Confusion	Uncooperative	Muscle tension
Anger	Accident-prone	Headaches
Irritability	Procrastination	Sleeplessness
Paranoia	On tranquillisers	Frequent colds
Mood changes	Eating disorders	Stomach ache
Guilt	Absenteeism	Nausea
Sexual temptation	Sexual licence	Sexual disease

Many of these signs are common to normal life, and could easily provoke introspection and hypochondria if they were all treated equally seriously! Many only become significant indicators of stress when they appear to an unusual degree or if several appear simultaneously.

The origin of stress

There is a difference between knowing the source of something and its origin. The source of coffee may be a percolator, but its origin is the bean from the coffee bush. For practical purposes, knowing the sources of stress may be sufficient in helping us to deal with them; but to truly understand our position as human beings, it is vital to know the means by which stress came into being.

In the modern scientific world we are told that the origin of stress lies in some notion of the evolutionary imperative. Stress is here to sort out the fit from the unfit, to carry on the relentless task of perfecting the human race by selecting out those who are less well adapted to survive the harsh realities of competitive pressures. Alternatively, we may be asked to believe that the true origin of stress lies in understanding our biochemistry. Subtle chemical and hormonal changes may offer clues to the fluctuations in our ability to tolerate stress.

However, while evolutionary theory and biochemical research may offer us insights into stress, they still only inform us about its sources rather than its origin. Only the Scriptures can offer an explanation. Turning to them, we discover that the real origin of stress is rooted in God. Conflict, pain and alienation did not just happen – it was brought about by Adam and Eve's rebellion against him and his consequent punishment. In a sense, therefore, the origin of stress is God. The main focus of the fall is not sociological (humanity's stressful relationship with society) but theological (humanity's broken relationship with God). It is not about what we experience (conflict, pain and alienation) but about what God has done (banishment). The question is not how we cope with stress, but rather how we find someone to save us from our helpless state before God.

The idea that the origin of stress is God's righteous punishment permeates Scripture:

There the Lord will give you an anxious mind, eyes weary with longing, and a despairing heart. You will live in constant suspense, filled with dread both night and day, never sure of your life. In the morning you will say, "If only it were evening!" and in the evening, "If only it were morning!" – because of the terror that will fill your hearts and the sights that your eyes will see. *Deuteronomy 28:65–67*

For the creation was subjected to frustration, not by its own choice, but by the will of the one who subjected it, in hope that the creation itself will be liberated from its bondage to decay and brought into the glorious freedom of the children of God. *Romans 8:20–21*

It is not fashionable in contemporary society to concede that God punishes humankind. We feel more comfortable with a God who is endlessly understanding in ineffectual benevolence. But Scripture teaches that God is angered at our rebellion and will, if necessary, take severe action, even it means excluding us from paradise.

The origin of stress, therefore, does not lie in the twenty-first century, nor in pace or populousness, nor in additives or negativities, nor in pollution or poverty. Stress originates in God's righteous punishment, and only he is able to deal with it. Only he can act on our behalf to save us from the eternal sentence he has imposed on our broken faith. Only he can act on our behalf to save us from the stress we experience in this life as part of the righteous punishment we all face. We can only look to him to exercise mercy and grace towards each of us individually. Without that, we are lost. Our hope rests on Jesus and his completed work on our behalf on the cross.

STRESS AT WORK

A daughter saw her dad returning home one evening with piles of files. She asked her mother, 'Why is Daddy always bringing home work?'

Her mother replied, 'Because he can't finish it in the office.'

'Why doesn't he join a slower group then?'

These days, pressure, promotion and yet more pressure seems inevitable 'Whoever wants a quiet life', suggested Tolstoy, 'is living in the wrong generation.' It has been estimated that 30–40 per cent of all absence from work due to sickness is attributable to some form of emotional disturbance. Absenteeism costs business in the UK £11 billion a year, of which 30 per cent is stress-related. The Cambridge University Centre for Brain Repair reports that stress can trigger changes in genes and in hormone levels, which precipitate dysfunction. Organisational structures, job designs, the incessant need to travel, compulsory redundancy, short-term contracts, badly managed workloads and relentless targets all bear some blame. We have already noted how stress is built into human existence, indeed that God has ordered it as part of his righteous punishment. But all too commonly we exacerbate the stress in our lives and our work by wilful and misguided patterns of behaviour. We will now look at how we ourselves may sometimes bring about even more conflict, pain and alienation.

Almost everyone agrees that work is more stressful than it ought to be. Speaking to a group of businessmen on the subject on one occasion, I discovered that there was widespread regret that their work came at such a price. Yet the majority of these people were not helpless juniors: some of them were the most senior and influential members of their organisations. The price of corporate profitability, career progression and a rising income was high, but it seemed inevitable. A recent survey by the pressure group, Parents at Work, revealed that 40 per cent of their respondents attributed the main cause of excessive hours at work to poor organisation. However, 70 per cent would do nothing about it if they had their time again. This may be because 50 per cent of the respondents accepted excessive hours as the price of personal advancement. For others, there was little else in their lives.

Stress can also derive from boredom, routine and isolation. If work is excessively fragmented, the creative elements of planning, performing and reviewing become dislocated. Certain workers are then left with just the dismal donkey work

> So I hated life, because the work that is done under the sun was grievous to me. All of it is meaningless, a chasing after the wind. I hated all the things I had toiled for under the sun, because I must leave them to the one who comes after me. And who knows whether he will be a wise man or a fool? Yet he will have control over all the work into which I have poured my effort and skill ... So my heart began to despair over all my toilsome labour under the sun. For a man may do his work with wisdom, knowledge and skill, and then he must leave all he owns to someone who has not worked for it. This too is meaningless and a great misfortune. What does a man get for all the toil and anxious striving with which he labours under the sun? All his days his work is pain and grief; even at night his mind does not rest. This too is meaningless. *Ecclesiastes 2:17–23*

Three aspects of stressful toil warrant closer examination – long hours, inadequate rest and poor leisure. The question we will be asking throughout is, are these all inevitable?

Long hours

An average working week might add up to 40–50 hours. Research has indicated that chief executive officers (CEOs) in the USA spend 12.9 hours per day, 6 days per week on their job – that's 77 hours per week. In the UK, the figures are 14.5 hours over 6.5 days – 95 hours per week. It would be rash for me to comment on whether the tasks facing CEOs really warrant such a commitment. And indeed, people's levels of mental and physical stamina may vary enough to make legalistic generalisations about what constitutes 'long hours' inappropriate.

It is flattering to be indispensable. Few of those working 70+ hrs per week are embarrassed by the culture they are helping to create: on the contrary, they wear it as a flag of their achievement. A training manager in a large multinational computer company revealed to me that he rarely saw his children because he never left work before 8 pm. I sympathised. Then, later, he remarked on the inefficient use of time in his company, partly due to the peaks and troughs of training activities. I asked him what he did on the lighter days. He said the company routine was always the same. At 6 pm everyone would break for a coffee. If they were busy, this would be perfunctory. If not, they would sit on each other's desks and chat – about work, news or the family. This might last an hour or more, after which they would work until 8 pm, setting themselves up for the next day. Company culture prevented anyone leaving before 8 pm. He argued that it would show lack of commitment. Should we sympathise with *that*?

Another aspect of long hours is the commute. Television documentaries have drawn our attention to the phenomenon of commuters who work in London but live in Doncaster, Bournemouth and Bristol. A few travel even greater distances, undertaking journeys of over two hours a day each way. Car journeys of 60 miles each way are not inconceivable. One can only wonder what costs are incurred in energy consumption and environmental pollution to meet this demand. We are told that these journeys provide an opportunity for reading (in the train, not the car!) and relaxation, for preparation and unwinding. They permit a wonderful weekend in the country, and offer the scope to live in housing the like of which would be unthinkable nearer London. But other issues arise, particularly in relation to the integrated lifestyle.

Colleagues at the same workplace can live hundreds of miles away from each other. The chances of developing relationships, where colleagues can also be friends, neighbours, spouses, sports club opponents, church members or school governors, are small. A community takes on the aspect of a dormitory town since this is essentially what the exhausted commuter requires after a punishing week at work. The contribution such a person can make to community life will not be great.

A variation on this theme is the weekly commuter. On one occasion I needed to meet the representative of a national institute who had distinguished himself in its service. It quickly emerged that his family lived in the West Country while he worked in London. He tried to get home each weekend, but this was fast becoming less of a routine – on reflection, it was averaging about two weekends a month. Even when he did make it home, he did not arrive until very late on Friday night. When this 'phase' was over, he intended to have a good break with the family!

Many will argue that working long hours is a matter of personal choice – it harms no one, and therefore we should live and let live. But this is clearly untrue. Some restaurants claim to have smoking and non-smoking areas. They do not seem to have grasped that smoke travels and, by giving someone the right to smoke, you effectively extinguish the right of another to enjoy a smoke-free meal. The 'long-hours merchant' contributes to a culture that makes moderation difficult to achieve for others. I have worked with colleagues who have a limited family life and approach work both as employment and hobby. An email sent at 1 am on a Saturday is seen as an amusing signal of dedication. But is this just a matter of individual taste?

In the film *Parenthood* we see promotion being given not to the loyal, hard-working, family man (Steve Martin) but to the company slave who tramples on relationships, pollutes business ethics and worships 'closing the deal' above everything else. Anyone lured by the success of this choice must face the implications not only for the working culture and other colleagues but also for the family. As this becomes more extreme, their actions have implications for relationships and the community. The cost of divorce is high – for the children, friends and relations. The whole community must adapt to the new, separated units, not knowing whether to 'take sides'.

The process of severing a marriage soaks up counselling, social, legal and judicial resources to achieve the desired end. A personnel management journal has claimed that the costs of divorce to the organisation are about £5,000 per individual. This was an attempt to quantify the effects of ill-health, hospitalisation, liver cirrhosis, absenteeism, depression, financial problems and the decreased life expectancy which apparently accompany divorce, especially for men. Small wonder that the Lord God states emphatically, 'I hate divorce' (Mal 2:16). Research now shows that divorce in the office appears to be contagious, setting a precedent for others to launch out on 'a new start'.

What of the future? Few people now talk about labour-saving devices. The pressures of working life have scarcely been alleviated by mobile telephones designed to keep you in touch even when you are out, or answering machines designed to keep people at bay even when you are in. High-speed trains and the Internet have had the same effect in the working world as new technologies and lightweight materials have had in the mountaineering world – they help you take on more. What they do not do is allow you to take on less. We have to develop a taste for roundedness and balance before 'more' ceases to be equated with 'better'. We have to be willing to learn from perspectives in the developing world, where poverty in relationships is regarded as a wasting disease and where some Western societies are seen as gripped by relentless famine.

Nearly three thousand years ago, the prophet Amos alerted us to the connection between workaholism and deteriorating standards of integrity at work:

> Hear this, you who trample the needy
>   and do away with the poor of the land, saying,
> 'When will the New Moon be over
>   that we may sell grain,
> and the Sabbath be ended
>   that we may market wheat?' –
> skimping the measure,
>   boosting the price
>   and cheating with dishonest scales,
> buying the poor with silver
>   and the needy for a pair of sandals,
>   selling even the sweepings with the wheat. *Amos 8:4–6*

Spectacular dishonesties now emerge with dispiriting frequency in junk bonds, insider share deals, public service contracts, mis-stated corporate accounts and company takeovers. Perhaps it is obvious that if profits are important enough to sacrifice more and more time, a few short cuts can surely be worth the risk. In Amos's time, the marketplace was infested with traders who could not abide bank holidays and weekends. Few today would argue that standards of integrity in the UK economy are as high as they were only a generation ago.

Incorporating plenty of rest and leisure is a good indicator of a healthy perspective to life. Here are some questions we might ask ourselves when thinking about the hours we commit to work:

- Do we really need to undertake all the tasks we have in mind, or can we delegate some responsibilities to someone else?

- Have we actually determined the number of hours (including commuting) we are prepared to put into our work, or do we merely bob about like a cork on a wave of expediency?

- Besides the financial considerations, do we take account of our interest in the job, personal temperament, community responsibilities, health and stamina?

- Do those most affected by our decision to work longer hours genuinely support that decision, or are they simply being loyal despite it?

Inadequate rest

A generation ago, even if a family only attended church for births, deaths and marriages, they would not have given a second thought as to how they would spend Sunday: it was the day of rest for the whole family. If they could afford it, a roast dinner would be popped into the oven with a milk pudding. It might cost a little more but it was an easy meal to prepare and filled the house with a warming aroma. Late mornings, lazy breakfasts, leisurely newspapers, large lunches, light walks and loquacious chatter among the in-laws and out-laws were taken for granted, as most of our precious privileges are until we find them under threat of disappearing forever.

Then suddenly, without warning, the government invited Robin Auld, QC, to present a report on the confused state of Sunday trading laws. He calmly recommended the abolition, in England, Wales and Scotland, of all legal restrictions on shops remaining open. He dismissed all alternatives to this astonishing approach as unworkable, because they would not form the basis of a fair, simple and readily enforceable system. One wag observed that on this basis we would need to abolish the tax system.

In February 1983, David Mellor, the Home Office minister, told the House of Commons about the possibility of reform, and added, 'The decision must be for the individual conscience of Honourable Members.' This was no great surprise, in view of the clear moral and religious overtones surrounding the subject. The problem was not in dispute – the law was archaic and anomalous, and needed reform. The government's solution was bound to need sensitive handling, and not just because of moral and religious implications. Culturally, under attack were centuries of British tradition going back, beyond the Fairs and Markets Act of 1448, to restrictions on Sunday trading established in King Athelstan's reign c. AD 940. Socially, the disturbance to all those living near shops would be bound to attract protest. Ethically, it was bound to damage the career of anyone with conscientious objections to working on Sunday, such as the Olympic athlete Eric Liddell, whose story is told in the film Chariots of Fire. Politically, the consequences of deregulation were far-reaching: 2.2 million people worked in the retail trade alone, half of them married women. It would have enormous implications for those required to provide the infrastructure for the millions of extra working days per month, such as the transport industry, distributive trades, police, catering and waste disposal, to name but a few.

Spiritually, corporate Sunday worship for the Christian family would be undermined.

All kinds of polls were produced, which only served to show that people could be persuaded to say 'yes' to almost anything, provided it sounded positive, implied no consequences, and was not obviously contradicted by their previous answer. However, one Harris Poll in 1986 stands out: it showed that 93 per cent of the population wanted the right not to work on Sunday if they wished. What might not have been immediately obvious, of course, was that if no regulations existed then some would choose to work, thus setting up a commercial domino effect. The John Lewis Partnership illustrated the point well in their evidence to the Home Office: if a football spectator stood up in his seat at the stadium, he would immediately gain a better view. But, to redress the balance, the spectators behind him would have to stand up. Soon anyone who wanted to see the game would have to stand up, so they would then be back where they started, with one difference – now they were all standing, whereas previously they were all sitting comfortably.

The government proceeded to achieve what had seemed impossible – it succeeded in uniting the church. Strange bedfellows they may have been, but several denominations found themselves in an alliance with MPs of all parties, trade unions, most small retailers, some major retailers and the National Chamber of Trade. Despite a massive parliamentary majority, the government decided to impose a three-line whip on the vote in April 1986, but they still suffered their first significant defeat since the previous election.

Some time later, I discussed the subject with Norman Lamont, my MP, in a Saturday surgery. He seemed bewildered by all the fuss. I urged him to press for a creative reform of the law so that its sound principles could be given practical credibility over future decades. But he indicated that the cabinet was unlikely to pick up that political 'hot potato' again in the near future. If only he had been right. Two years later, in 1991, certain major supermarket chains defiantly announced that they would trade on the Sundays leading up to Christmas – 'for the convenience of customers'. They made this announcement in November in the hope of catching their competitors off guard. Their directors knew that the government wanted to abolish restrictions on Sunday trading, and abolition by disregard is as effective as abolition by legislation.

The Attorney General announced that there was no intention of the government intervening. On 1 December, John Gummer MP stated on Radio 4 that it would be 'immoral' for the government to enforce a law the contents of which were unclear. A law which had been passably clear in its principles for more than three decades was now publicly emasculated shortly after the government had failed to repeal it. Our civic leaders abdicated their duty.

How important is this issue? Can the tiny minority of Christians in this country expect the rest of the population, of different faiths and no faith, to conform to an outmoded tradition? Is it realistic for a modern industrial society to take seriously dated biblical teaching given to an ancient people? It is partly because of the clarity of the Scriptures on this issue that such a consensus has emerged among the churches. Even the most cursory reader of the Bible could not fail to see the thrust of God's mind on the principle of rest.

God set us his example by resting on the seventh day of Creation (Gen 2:2), thus establishing the principle of one day's rest in seven as part of his work of creation. He then enshrined that principle in the Ten Commandments (Exod 20:8–11). In what is the most detailed of all his command-ments, he reaffirmed the basis of the principle as a creation ordinance (v 11). When the commandment is restated in Deuteronomy, a complementary reason is given for having it: not only is it a remembrance of creation, but also of

Exodus – that outstanding act of deliverance by God in the Old Testament (Deut 5:12–15).

After the resurrection of Christ, the observance of this principle shifted from Saturday to Sunday, to reflect this new, supreme demonstration of God's power to deliver. In other words, the day of rest celebrates both an eternal principle established at creation and the unique redemption displayed at the resurrection. Creation and redemption – these are the themes that underpin biblical thinking on setting aside one day in seven for rest. God even defines its parameters: 'you shall not do any work, neither you, nor your son or daughter, nor your manservant or your maidservant, nor your ox, your donkey or any of your animals, nor the alien within your gates' (v 14). No one is exempt. Rest is a human right, not a religious rite. The God of the whole earth ordains it *for everyone*, not just for his chosen people alone.

In the centuries after Moses brought them God's law, the more perceptive among his people could not fail to appreciate the seriousness of his plainly stated view. The principle of rest was a sign of the covenant between them and God (Exod 31:12–13), just like a wedding ring is more than a piece of costume jewellery between husband and wife. Its observance or breach served as a barometer for the spiritual health or malaise of the whole nation, and seemed to be associated with their general prosperity or adversity (Isa 58:13–14).

In his day, Nehemiah, the governor of Jerusalem, did not hesitate to confront the DIY entrepreneurs of his day who were intent on disregarding the Sabbath regulations (Neh 13:1–22). They may well have been able to absorb the fines incurred and still laugh all the way to the bank, so Nehemiah took decisive steps to uphold his social responsibilities as governor. He gathered convincing evidence. He issued a formal warning. He rebuked the civic leaders for abdicating their duty to lead. Doubtless this won him few friends, but when no response was evident he courted even greater unpopularity by closing down the customs and excise function on the Sabbath, effectively blocking the movement of goods into the city.

The traders demonstrated their fury by staging a sit-in at the closed checkpoint. No doubt the city hacks had plenty to say in their morning editions, about restraint of trade, inadequate consultations, business freedoms, increased efficiency in the retail sector and the minor inconvenience suffered by the vocal minority who wanted to make criminals out of honest workers. The Jerusalem public waited to see who would back down first in this confrontation between big business and the rule of law. Finally, the governor put his future on the line – he threatened to arrest the traders if they persisted in civil disobedience. Bewildered by his unwillingness to compromise, their bravado melted away. Nehemiah's society was fortunate indeed to have a politician of such vision and courage.

The stark truth is that if the church does not defend the principle of one day of rest each week, nobody else will. There are many today whose entire approach to life is based on expediency. Such people are acquiescing in the slide towards increased levels of stress in society and the deterioration in the sustainable quality of life. They probably believe they are marching under the banner of freedom. They may find, however, that they will enjoy the benefit of Sunday rest for a shorter period than they had imagined. The historic events leading to the abolition of restrictions on Sunday trading were undoubtedly in tune with the unrestrained commercialism of our society, but they will never be in tune with God's desire for the well-being of ordinary people and their families.

We need a politician of Nehemiah's stature to push this issue back on the agenda. It may currently be a political non-starter, but for some of us acquiescence is also a non-starter. Perhaps we should ask ourselves:

- How committed are we really to the fourth commandment?
- Do we value sufficiently the rhythm of rest?
- How can we use rest creatively?
- How will we act, now that the forces of commercialism have achieved the almost total deregulation of Sunday trading?

Poor leisure

I have no idea how television viewing hours are calculated but, if statistics are to be believed, a very large number of people spend a very large proportion of their leisure hours sitting passively in front of the box. Elsewhere, crowds congregate to shout support for their heroes on the stage or pitch. For others, work dominates and sleep is the main alternative activity. A church variation on this is the six-evenings-a-week ministry activist, charging like a holy cow through a never-ending schedule of Bible studies, prayer meetings, evangelism and parish committees.

People's leisure time can also be taken up with consumption, whether it be non-stop partying with drink, drugs, sex and music to stimulate the bored and boring, or the lavish and repeated 'need' for corporate entertainment. Even shopping has been elevated beyond the purchase of goods required. The decor, lighting, displays, integral coffee shops, indoor plants, cascading water and live music from a genuine Bechstein – these are designed to make shopping a soothing and meaningful experience. The purchase is almost incidental. But will such mindless passivity and relentless consumption offer the quality of leisure adequate to meet the needs of today's pressured lifestyle? Certainly our leisure choices are revealing, because they indicate the value we place on matters that are uniquely within our influence. C S Lewis puts it uncompromisingly: 'Our leisure, even our play, is a matter of serious concern. There is no neutral ground in the universe; every square inch, every split second, is claimed by God and counter claimed by Satan.' Rest is God's framework within which to build leisure. Leisure and play should be seen as the creative use of rest rather than elevated to an importance they do not warrant. What is the place of leisure when many do not take up their full annual leave entitlement?

Watching a child play imaginatively is like watching a butterfly in summer – something very precious. Here is inspiration and the carefree which cannot be captured and bottled. But, with the passage of time, we gradually see the inspiration replaced by calculation and the carefree pushed aside by the careworn. Parents may even hasten this process. Educational activities, purposeful hobbies, intellectual games, sports matches and endless music practice over weekends to pass grades can become a child's route to premature workaholism. If all that matters is effectiveness and efficiency, how will we cultivate vision and inspiration in our society?

In biblical thinking, leisure is linked with feasting and communal celebration. For God's people, rest, leisure, music, food, drink and companionship were associated with celebrating significant religious events and with worship. 'In Israel, as in all nations, there was a host of feasts which, though they did not celebrate a religious event, had a religious character' (Roland de Vaux). Celebration could not be divorced from faith:

> The child grew and was weaned, and on the day Isaac was weaned Abraham held a great feast. *Genesis 21:8*

> Then Miriam the prophetess, Aaron's sister, took a tambourine in her hand, and all the women followed her, with tambourines and dancing. Miriam sang to them:

'Sing to the Lord,
    for he is highly exalted…' *Exodus 15:20–21*

For the Jews it was a time of happiness and joy, gladness and honour. In every province and in every city, wherever the edict of the king went, there was joy and gladness among the Jews, with feasting and celebrating. *Esther 8:16,17*

Jesus also recognised the value of leisure and enjoying oneself. His first miracle was to enlarge the supply of wine at a wedding breakfast: 'He thus revealed his glory' (John 2:11). His parables often centred on or concluded with feasting and celebration (eg Matt 22:1–14; 25:1–13; Luke 15:1–32). Some even criticised him for not being ascetic enough (Matt 11:19). Evidently the religious killjoys did not welcome a spirituality that took pleasure in the body and leisure.

Leland Ryken highlights the *joie de vivre* in Jesus' sense of humour:

The giantesque, the hilarious exaggeration, the preposterous fantasy. There is present in the humour of Christ the same spirit that underlies much leisure. That spirit is characterised by such qualities as nonseriousness, a letting go of formality and inhibition, high-spiritedness, and spontaneity.

Humour lightens and adorns our leisure, and too many Christians are conspicuously un-Christlike in this respect.

Jesus took steps to ensure that his disciples had some time away from the hurly-burly (Mark 6:31). We, too, would do well to cultivate our leisure: active diversions for the desk-bound, unstructured fun for the filofaxed, gentle merriment for the manual worker, spontaneity for the duty-ridden. Here again, children are our best tutors. Recreation occurs when children 'recreate' roles that are not their own, and 'travel far from home' in complete safety to explore the world of cops and robbers, doctors and nurses, mums and dads, engine drivers, teachers and soldiers. Likewise, rest and recreation for adults are often associated with role reversal and exploration – the weekend paintball manoeuvres, singing in a choir, or amateur dramatics.

Without worshipping the weekend, there is a case for arguing that more prominence should be given to quality leisure, carefree play, family fun and memorable role-recreation as part of the rhythm of rest and work. We should ask ourselves the following:

- What moral values are revealed by your leisure choices?

- Do they offer you contrast, variety, refreshment and fun amidst necessary responsibilities?

- When did you last spend time in leisure with your friends?

- Do your children or grandchildren have enough space for imaginative, unstructured play?

- Are landmarks in the life of your family adequately cemented into the family 'story' by celebration?

COPING WITH STRESS

Our society is moving at an astonishing pace. It has been estimated that within the next decade 50 per cent of the workforce will occupy jobs that do not currently exist. Within the next half-century, 97 per cent of all recorded information will have been acquired in the last fifty years. Unless we begin to take seriously the importance of finding islands of stability and rest amidst all this turbulence, we will be unable to prevent ourselves from being spun like a top throughout our lives.

Perhaps the most difficult part of stress, even after we have understood a little more about it, is to know how to set about recovering a modicum of rest. We will look now at some possible ways of coping with stress.

Coping with conflict

Resolving conflict in personal relationships requires a range of interpersonal skills such as being able to listen, consult, negotiate, persuade, rebuke, and give and receive feedback. Having a sense of humour also helps to keep things in perspective, and being able to read non-verbal signals. Each of us may possess these skills in greater measure than we realise, and we can build on them by learning from experience and through training. There are many benefits to be gained by acquiring skills in conflict resolution and reconciliation. Companies will often provide opportunities for this, and will have established procedures for consultation, staff develop-ment, and handling grievances and other disciplinary matters.

Scripture has some very practical advice to offer on dealing with conflict:

> Do not repay anyone evil for evil. Be careful to do what is right in the eyes of everybody. If it is possible, as far it depends on you, live at peace with everyone. *Romans 12:17–18*

Christians especially should aim high and exercise forbear-ance, even under heavy provocation. We should be careful, though, not to become paranoid and imagine that there will always be someone who is out to get us and pull down our faith. Occasionally, the proper response to conflict requires that we identify the specific source of a problem and deal with it. But even then we should avoid the natural tempta-tion to retaliate, which invariably inflames matters.

The passage also enjoins us 'to do what is right in the eyes of everybody'. A senior manager of a City business once told me of an occasion when he had felt that acquiescing to a particular course of action would lead someone else, quite wrongly, to believe he had fiddled his expenses. He quickly took the opportunity to interrupt the flow of conversation and correct this view. Even the appearance of evil must be challenged.

However, Scripture is not so naive as to believe that simply trying hard will resolve problems of conflict with uncooperative people. There will be those who are impossible, who will want a fight, to hurt another deeply, to win at any cost. One of the most gentle and kind families we know was forced to move house because of a dispute with a neighbour. How that neighbour managed to generate a fight with them at all remains a complete mystery to me. So while we should seek to 'live at peace with everyone', it is only 'as far as it depends on' us. After all, for no apparent reason, it is sometimes the case that 'the wicked lie in wait for the righteous, seeking their very lives' (Ps 37:32)

Some key principles for dealing with conflict at work can be gleaned from the words of Jesus:

> 'If your brother sins against you, go and show him his fault, just between the two of you. If he listens to you, you have won your brother over. But if he will not listen, take one or two others along, so that "every matter may be established by the testimony of two or three witnesses." If he refuses to listen to them, tell it to the church; and if he refuses to listen even to the church, treat him as you would a pagan or a tax collector.' *Matthew 18:15–17*

- Take the initiative. It is always tempting to feel that, as the aggrieved party, you have no responsibility but to wait for an apology or justice.
- If possible, keep a disagreement with someone else to yourself and that person. Don't try to get

others on your side by telling all and sundry. Conflict is hardly ever resolved by threatening another person's dignity, however much fun this may appear to be. Publicity and self-justification harden lines quickly.

- Keep everything fairly low key. Setting things down formally in writing is only worth doing if your aim is to protect your future interests, and will only serve to goad the other towards crisis. Quiet confidentiality can save face and minimise the cost of resolution.

- Be prepared to prove your point. It is not enough to just to cry about your feelings. You need to gather evidence and give reasons to support your view.

- Be prepared to take serious matters further. While it is unwise to rush to adopt a full frontal approach to conflict, and no one will take seriously someone who overreacts to every slight, when a deep-rooted conflict is damaging relationships and performance in the workplace, we should be prepared to go through with the unpleasantness of a formal hearing and involving others.

- Accept that dismissal or resignation may be the only solution for you or your adversary.

Such principles are often enshrined in good procedures for resolving grievances in organisations.

While senior managers must take ultimate responsibility for resolving conflicts in the workplace and making hard decisions in the interests of the staff and the business, we should all place a high value on good quality working relationships and be prepared to bend over backwards to achieve them. In the final analysis, the whole viability of a department, or indeed of a whole company, can be called into question if the boil is not lanced.

Sometimes, however, we will simply have to learn to live with injustice. Not all of us will occupy a senior position, and only an idealist believes that success always attends sincerity. A senior manager may sometimes be unwilling to take further action, and it then becomes counterproductive to press on. After single-minded and conscientious efforts at finding solutions have failed, we may sometimes simply have to let it go and endure. We need great wisdom in determining when to settle a conflict and when to bow out gracefully. These matters do not always depend on us, and this may be difficult to face. In the end we may have to live with injustice, especially if it is covert and inflicted by someone in a powerful position.

I speak from experience as one who has been at the receiving end of oppressive behaviour – the constant recourse to blame and intimidation, using organisational restructuring to settle scores, the displays of staggering self-confidence, suppurating weakness and vanity masquerading as decisive toughness. In the workplace there is often no need to provoke malice – it arises all by itself. It is astonishing the treachery you will encounter in work cultures marked by ingratitude and lack of trust. And this has always been true. I wonder whether David wrote Psalms 140–143 when he faced such a time. I have found that these psalms perfectly express the anguish and turmoil I have passed through more than once.

It is thought that these psalms were written against the backdrop of David's encounter with the citizens of Keilah (1 Sam 23). Violent intent, poisonous lips, hidden snares (Ps 140:1–3) – these, it seemed, were the hallmarks of the Keilahite culture. David had risked both himself and his army to go to the city's aid when it was under attack from the Philistines. He had won a stunning victory and rescued Keilah's women and children from the unspeakable consequences of defeat. Meanwhile, King Saul, David's erstwhile mentor and now sworn enemy, learned that the his quarry was in Keilah and that he now had an opportunity to capture David and kill him. David learned of Saul's plan and, as always, turned to God for help. He asked God, 'Will the citizens of Keilah surrender me and my men to Saul?' – a strange question to ask about a people whom he had only recently rescued from wipeout. But God's answer was unequivocal: 'They will.'

To describe enduring oppressive behaviour as a coping strategy belies the effort involved. It is one thing to know that the Lord secures justice, another to set a guard over your mouth when you want to give vent to your thoughts (Ps 141:3,4). It is one thing to fix your eyes on the Sovereign Lord, another not to feel completely overcome with despair (v 8). When you grow faint, no one offers any concern, and you know you are facing stronger opponents – all you can do is cry out to God (Ps 142:1–4). Under pressure we will be tempted to say and do things we regret, but God sees beyond the surface and will recognise our utter despair. His unfailing love will act to guide, rescue, teach and lead us out of the dark night of our despair (Ps 143:8–10).

Coping with pain

Helping their staff avoid stress is a matter that has gone to the top of the agenda for employers in the wake of recent case law that suggests that they may be liable to pay damages for overburdening their staff while offering inadequate support. Staff can help themselves avoid the pain of work pressures by, for example, adopting rational planning of work, such as maintaining clear diary arrangements, coming properly prepared for daily tasks and delegating appropriately to colleagues. For organisations, rational planning may mean involving staff as widely as possible in working out the implications of pursuing company objectives; ensuring they have ready access to the resources they need to succeed; and striking a balance between comprehensive discussion and speedy action, individual preferences and collective concerns, competition and cooperation, the needs of colleagues and the needs of the organisation.

A healthy lifestyle is another weapon against stress. Individuals should take responsibility for ensuring they watch their diet and take regular exercise, as well as taking time off for rest and leisure. Weekends, evenings, holiday breaks and timetables may all need to be reviewed and priorities identified. You may be called upon to make hard choices both at work and at home. The ability to say no, and stick to it, could be the most effective weapon of all.

It is often easy to miss the blindingly obvious when you never pause long enough to feel exhausted and depressed. Elijah discovered this when he attempted to take on the entire political and religious establishment of his day (1 Kings 18:1 – 19:18) and he was in the minority of one. Imagine the tension, the sleepless build-up in the days and weeks beforehand. When the clash arrived, Elijah endured the appalling confrontation and taunts from morning to twilight. Even success brought no rest – he found himself forced to flee into the desert, with a price on his head. Overarching all these physical and mental stresses was the profound spiritual battle in which he was engaged. No wonder he reached the point of collapse. But God intervened, and what did he do for Elijah? Prescribe deep counselling? Offer profound words of spiritual comfort? No – he provided sleep, food and drink, followed by more sleep, food and drink. Here is the intersecting point at which the practical and the spiritual meet.

There are many books available in good bookshops offering guidance on these issues. Christians would be as foolish to dismiss the fruits of modern research into stress at work as they would be to opt for prayer alone, without anaesthetic, prior to surgery. The best approach is to have the best of both worlds: to embrace the insights of research (where these are consistent with biblical faith) while maintaining a distinctive Christian framework in which those insights can be measured against God's revelation.

Coping with alienation

Alienation seems to be more difficult to resolve. The most important resource we can draw on is Scripture. Only a consistent and growing study of God's Word will lead us to sound beliefs and a balanced perspective on life. The world's views, cut off from revelation, inevitably lead to alienation and imbalance. Building relationships in the church fellowship, the home and the community can help us to recover a positive perspective, suggest fresh solutions and reaffirm our personal worth in the face of discouragement.

At work, alienation can be countered by looking again at the values underpinning an organisation: whether it encourages teamwork, involves staff in decision-making, holds regular performance appraisals, identifies new targets and agrees ways to enhance personal development. If you think you are feeling alienated because your own values are distorted, some heart-searching and reflection may be appropriate. This may lead you to rethink your direction in life and undertake a more mature, gentler assessment of your achievements. In short, core values may need to be re-stated as you are 'transformed by the renewing of your mind' (Rom 12:2).

In one organisation I worked for, a CBI communications audit revealed one of the highest scores ever recorded relating to job satisfaction. However, the same audit also showed low morale. In other words, the staff believed that their work was worthwhile and important to the community, and that they were well suited to meet its challenges; but when they considered their pay levels and the negative publicity associated with their area of work, they felt undervalued and discouraged. In these circumstances, it seems to me that one should change one's assessment and stand by the worthwhile work, refusing to be pressured by the false and fickle fashions of public popularity. Fashions and governments change.

On the other hand, your values may be sound as a bell but you may be operating in a company culture that is hostile to your cherished priorities. Naturally, there may be times when we should attempt to change the culture, since we are a component of it as much as anyone else is. If this fails, and the sense of alienation persists, perhaps on reflection it may be right to take the extreme course of moving jobs or career with all that this entails in terms of relocation and retraining. It takes courage to embark on a new journey, particularly when your feelings may be at an all time low.

'Is any one among you in trouble? He should pray' (James 5:13). For the Christian, prayer is the key factor in managing stress. God has invited us to come to him and find rest in a world that he knows is wearisome beyond our endurance at times. This will come as a rebuke to many Christians whose daily dilemmas at work hardly rate a mention in prayer. When we face trouble at work, our faith may all too often seem irrelevant, but we should make those times a valuable spur to prayer, an acceptance that true rest can only be found in God.

> Do not be anxious about anything, but in everything, by prayer and petition, with thanksgiving, present your requests to God. And the peace of God, which transcends all understanding, will guard your hearts and your minds in Christ Jesus. *Philippians 4:6,7*

While it is encouraging to be reminded of the wide range of resources available for coping with stress, it is sobering to acknowledge how difficult it is in practice to put them together into an effective strategy. Managing stress is never a simple question of reacting with formulae. Indeed, as we have seen, sometimes stress simply has to be endured. However, at other times, its cause must be removed altogether. Coping with stress is very personal and requires a full awareness of an individual's circumstances. The effectiveness of coping strategies will depend on a sound analysis of the situation and a degree of maturity and self-knowledge. It can only be improved if you have the support of your church community, work colleagues or friends. You may also want to consider getting help through counselling (there are a growing number of well-qualified counsellors available), and literature and advice are available from Christian bookshops, GPs, health authorities, local libraries and community groups.

To seek help for stress is not defeatist or the outcome of having weak or incompetent staff. It may actually be a far-sighted attempt to find ways in which workers can perform at their best. Good management and stress management are closely related. Good managers are looked on by their staff as neither 'soft' or stressful to work for. They would not think of introducing new strategies and policies into the workplace without first assessing how much stress and resentment that will cause their staff. Coping strategies emerge most effectively when based on a proper audit of the actual problems and addressed through a tailored combination of appropriate counselling, training and preventive action.

'YOU WILL FIND REST FOR YOUR SOULS'

We said earlier that in one sense the origin of stress was God through his righteous punishment. The fundamental issue of banishment from Eden and God our Father cannot be avoided if human beings are to handle stress at a deep level. And we cannot resolve it alone: only God himself has provided the solution in Jesus, who gives rest to the weary and burdened (Matt 11:28–30). After Adam and Eve's expulsion from Eden, a flaming sword blocked the way back to our first home. We can never rest in peace until we return there at last. Jesus is the one to lead us back. He can only be God because no one else but God knows where paradise is. And, as he pilots us through the gates, the flaming sword falls on him – a blow that was unmistakably aimed at us. The tree of life becomes freely available to all who enter by this route. There is no other:

> 'I tell you the truth, the man who does not enter the sheep pen by the gate, but climbs in some other way, is a thief and a robber ... I tell you the truth, I am the gate for the sheep.'
> John 10:1,7

These are the living words of Jesus of Nazareth, God's Son, yet fully human, born of Mary, as demonstrated by his resurrection and ascension. There is no one else under heaven who can save us from the alienation we face outside paradise. If God had not intervened, there would be no remedy. The Christian response centres on him. It involves keeping in harmony with the Father, obeying his living Word and walking in step with his Holy Spirit. It means being committed to spending time with him and receiving rest as his gift. Scripture has faithfully delivered his message to us down the centuries:

'My Presence will go with you, and I will give you rest.'

Exodus 33:14

The Lord gave them rest on every side, just as he had sworn to their forefathers.   *Joshua 21:44*

But now the Lord my God has given me rest on every side, and there is no adversary or disaster.   *1 Kings 5:4*

My soul finds rest in God alone;
my salvation comes from him.   *Psalm 62:1*

If there was any doubt about this, the promise of Jesus himself is clear:

'Come to me, all you who are weary and burdened, and I will give you rest. Take my yoke upon you and learn from me, for I am gentle and humble in heart, and you will find rest for your souls.'   *Matthew 11:29*

SUMMARY

God's righteous punishment brings humanity into conflict, pain and alienation. It drives away that sense of rest for which we yearn. A truly Christian view of stress has to take account of the fall and God's righteous response to human disobedience. Only then is there a sound foundation for understanding stress and designing strategies to help us cope with it. The framework of conflict, pain and alienation provides a way of analysing the stress that hinders restfulness. It also enables the discoveries of science to be considered within a biblical framework.

Many Christians at work betray a willingness to stagger through life, burdened with long hours, inadequate rest and poor leisure. Though they claim to be victims, they may well have brought this burden upon themselves. Some of these matters are more within our control than we would like to concede. Those who believe that there is more to life than work, and being is just as important as doing, will find that thoughtful determination can roll back the stressful toil that clogs up our schedules. But we should put biblical convictions ahead of social conventions if we are to effect any progress in recovering rest in our lives. There is an exciting wholeness to recover in creative work and imaginative rest, as each accentuates the distinctive enjoyment that the other offers in terms of diversity and fullness of life.

Conflict, pain and alienation are bitter realities that can never be totally put right, but there are some things we can do about them. Conflict causes us difficulties with people, so developing better interpersonal skills will help. If conflict cannot be avoided, we may have to identify the specific cause of the conflict and deal realistically with that, as much as lies within our power. Occasionally we may have to accept that we will simply have to endure stress and rely on God's unfailing love to show us the way forward. Pain is debilitating, so we need to relax and pay careful attention to health and leisure. We may need to review our time commitments so that we can face up to our real priorities. Alienation may cause us to feel isolated and lost within the hostile environment in which we find ourselves outside Eden. Sometimes it is right to feel alienation from what is unacceptable. In certain areas we can alleviate our sense of alienation by seeking wise counsel, determining our core values or moving in new directions.

However, we cannot avoid the fact that we are banished from our first home and Father. Nor can we alone resolve this, for it originates in the righteous punishment of God. He himself alone has provided the solution in Jesus, who gives rest to the weary when they come to him in prayer. This rest cannot be bought or earned – it is a gift from God who gives it abundantly to those who ask.

Chapter 3

HARMONY

Employers and employees in productivity

How should a Christian be distinctive in the workplace? Is it by perpetually evangelising? By working hard and then, as a colleague of mine used to do, putting in some Bible reading at the desk during your free moments? Is it by being nicer than everyone else?

In this chapter we will be looking at how a Christian can be distinctive in the everyday work routine. While we should be prepared for more dramatic challenges in the workplace, most of our 90,000 hours there will consist of the fairly mundane. Yet the impact of these hours on our personal lives and on our productivity will largely depend on our fundamental attitude to being employed (paid or unpaid) and to employing others. The really unique worker is the one who remains buoyant and purposeful, day in, day out; who brings a transforming vitality to the daily routine without being worn out or discouraged. Even the mundane can present us with a challenge. In the pursuit of harmonious productivity, there is a constant need for creativity. Christians are called to 'be fruitful and increase in number' (Gen 1:28) and to be peacemakers (James 3:17–18). The work arena is a major opportunity to work this out in practice.

In New Testament times, it seems, work was taken for granted as the duty of every responsible citizen. In such an environment, church leaders tended to place greater emphasis on spreading the gospel, to ensure that the new imperatives for Christian discipleship were given their proper attention. Indeed, there seems to have been a super-spiritual lie doing the rounds, that work was unimportant in the final days leading up to Christ's return. Obviously, this was an attitude that Paul, in his letters to the early church, felt he needed emphatically to refute:

> Make it your ambition to lead a quiet life, to mind your own business and to work with your hands ... so that your daily life may win the respect of outsiders and so that you will not be dependent on anybody.   *1 Thessalonians 4:11,12*

> In the name of the Lord Jesus Christ, we command you, brothers, to keep away from every brother who is idle and does not live according to the teaching you received from us. For you yourselves know how you ought to follow our example. We were not idle when we were with you, nor did we eat anyone's food without paying for it. On the contrary, we worked night and day, labouring and toiling so that we would not be a burden to any of you. We did this, not because we do not have the right to such help, but in order to make ourselves a model for you to follow. For even when we were with you, we gave you this rule: 'If a man will not work, he shall not eat.'

> We hear that some among you are idle. They are not busy; they are busy-bodies. Such people we command and urge in the Lord Jesus Christ to settle down and earn the bread they eat.   *2 Thessalonians 3:6–12*

Paul was a champion of work, pouring scorn on 'idle busy-bodies' who were probably trying to make religion their excuse for avoiding it. As we have discovered so far from the passages from Genesis we looked at earlier, work is integral to human life, making idleness an aberration, a selfish form of inactivity, which is at best sterile. Those forced into inactivity – for example, through unemployment – often find themselves depressed and feeling that life has no purpose. A director of education, writing diffidently about his impending retirement, said, 'I cannot help wondering what life will be like without work, the great advantage of which is its contrast with non-work.' He did not seem to have yet developed a clear appreciation of the difference between retirement and inactivity.

In his play, *Uncle Vanya*, Chekhov paints a disturbing picture of a situation in which work is laid aside for too long. He powerfully evokes the therapeutic aspects of work, its cathartic and purposeful role, without which we would have nothing but aimlessness and futility. The celebrated Professor Serebryakov arrives back at the family estate. For twenty-five years, the play's protagonist, Vanya, has worshipped the professor's intellect and poured over his writings. Now that the professor has retired, all normal routines have been set aside in deference to him. Vanya observes, 'Only Sonya works and I just sleep, eat and drink. It's all wrong.'

Meanwhile, Dr Astrov is finding Serebryakov's beautiful young wife, Helen, at once irritating and tempting. He likewise finds himself abandoning the daily routine of work as he spends more and more time around her: 'For a whole month I do nothing at all, let everything slide because I simply have to see you.' But she herself suffers from too much leisure: 'She has no responsibilities and other people work for her. But there is something wrong with a life of idleness.' Later he says to her, 'You have nothing in the world to do, you may as well admit it – no object in life, nothing to occupy your mind – and sooner or later your feelings are going to be too much for you.' He accuses her: 'No sooner do you and your husband turn up in this place than people here who were getting on with their work, all busy creating something, have to drop everything and do nothing all summer but attend to you and your husband's gout. You two have infected us all with your idleness. If you'd stayed on here we'd have had a full-scale disaster on our hands.'

At the end of the drama, Serebryakov retreats from the moral lassitude he has brought upon everybody through his idleness, by exhorting them: 'You should get down to work, gentlemen. What we need is a bit of action.' Vanya, shattered by all that has happened, is also left looking to work for his salvation: 'I feel so depressed. I must get down to work quickly. To work then. Must work. Work – must work.' Chekhov acutely portrays how work gives shape to life and illusion leaves us rudderless.

In this chapter we will be looking at Paul's teaching about work to the early church. In particular, we will focus on the following verses from Ephesians, which are reiterated in Colossians:

Slaves, obey your earthly masters with respect and fear, and with sincerity of heart, just as you would obey Christ. Obey them not only to win their favour when their eye is on you, but like slaves of Christ, doing the will of God from your heart. Serve wholeheartedly, as if you were serving the Lord, not men, because you know that the Lord will reward everyone for whatever good he does, whether he is slave or free.

And masters, treat your slaves in the same way. Do not threaten them, since you know that he who is both their Master and yours is in heaven, and there is no favouritism with him.   *Ephesians 6:5–9*

Slaves, obey your earthly masters in everything; and do it, not only when their eye is on you and to win their favour, but with sincerity of heart and reverence for the Lord. Whatever you do, work at it with all your heart, as working for the Lord, not for men, since you know that you will receive an inheritance from the Lord as a reward. It is the

Lord Christ you are serving. Anyone who does wrong will be repaid for his wrong, and *there is no favouritism.*

Masters, provide your slaves with what is right and fair, because you know that you also have a Master in heaven.
Colossians 3:22 – 4:1

Paul lived in a society where slavery was commonplace, and his instructions to the church about work reflect this. Nevertheless, we cannot dismiss his teaching as relevant only to slaves and their masters, with nothing to say to workers in the twenty-first century. In fact, I would argue that it imposes upon us even higher standards. If Paul expected even Christian slaves to be conscientious in their work, how much more conscientious should Christian employees be as free workers in much less arduous contexts. And if Christian masters were required to be scrupulous in their treatment of their slaves, all the more should Christian employers adopt high standards of behaviour towards their staff.

Sooner or later, in any organisation, you will encounter truculence, confrontation, the pursuit of profit and power, lack of concern, divisiveness and injustice. Despite such provocations, it is contingent upon a Christian to seek to build harmony between employer and employee, and to strive for improvement and productivity in the interests of the organisation and its stakeholders.

THE CHRISTIAN EMPLOYEE

Four qualities emerge from these verses from Ephesians and Colossians, which should be innate to every Christian employee: his **approach** to work, his **attitude** to work, his **loyalty** to Christ and to his employer, and his **expectation** that he will reap what he has sown in relation to his work (Gal 6:7).

Approach

Like the first-century slave, the Christian employee should approach his work with an obedient and cooperative spirit. This implies having an attitude that is willing to listen and ready to act, obedient, respectful, reverent and sincere (Eph 6:5,6; Col 3:22). A cooperative spirit is rooted in a conscious acknowledgement that God has placed an individual in his or her position of responsibility, and that to cooperate in its fulfilment is to cooperate with him.

I once worked with a wonderful colleague who relished his supporting role. He gratuitously gave credit to his boss for his own achievements. He never chafed when instructions had to be reversed at the last minute. He was forceful in debate, but entirely relaxed when decisions went against him, and could always see merit in them. Among his own subordinates he was always positive about his boss and, when the latter left, organised a huge farewell party. His submission was strong, freely given and productive.

A cooperative spirit is at the opposite end of belligerence, manipulation, contempt and disloyalty; it stands out against the negativity, complaining and grumbling that taints many workplaces. It refuses to go along with the lampooning of management as if there were no complex decisions to be made or always scope to satisfy everyone. A cooperative spirit feels obliged to speak well of the organisation and is willing to take personal responsibility for the corporate reputation.

We should not confuse this attitude with mindless subservience. Some slaves in the ancient world occupied positions of immense power, and were highly valued and respected by their masters (see Gen 41:39–45; Dan 2:48,49). Any employer worth his or her salt will value constructive ideas, respectful questions and, in the right relationship, reasoned warnings against a course of action.

A cooperative spirit is rooted in a conscious acknowledgement of God's hand behind the office of responsibility: David recognized Saul's status as both his king and 'the Lord's anointed' (1 Sam 24:5,6), despite Saul's many faults and his unjust behaviour towards David himself. The Creator is committed to securing order, which, from time to time, is achieved by maintaining an undesirable status quo. It is certainly right that the occupant of high office should act with integrity, but even a vain and foolish boss is owed the duty of cooperation in the wider interests of order and stability in the community. Rebellion has often been dressed up as desire for justice. For the Christian, strike action against your employer – except in extreme circumstances as the lesser of two evils – will always raise fundamental questions that cannot easily be answered if respect for the office of manager is to be maintained. After all, these words of Scripture were first addressed to slaves.

Loyalty

A Christian's first loyalty is to Christ, and, from Paul's point of view, all Christian employees are actually employed by the Lord. It would not be too far-fetched to talk of all Christian workers as employees of Christ carrying out some aspect of his business plan. Work, therefore, is not a subsistence 'tentmaking' activity that Christians must undertake in order to finance their 'real work' in the church; neither is it a regrettable necessity or self-centred indulgence. The sacred/secular divide has been broken down. We are 'slaves of Christ', doing the will of God' and 'working for the Lord' (Eph 6:6; Col 3:23) and as such we should approach our work with energy, striving for excellence out of loyalty to him: 'everything that the slave now does is part of his new work for the Lord. He has been rescued at a stroke to become a full-time servant of Christ' (Dick Lucas).

Loyalty to the Lord may translate naturally into loyalty to the organisation, which is a company's richest asset, but its roots go much deeper. Such loyalty rests on the determination to build a firm foundation of integrity at the heart of an organisation and thereby to secure its long-term interests. Thus a company can be rescued from the temptation to put short-term expediency ahead of long-term credibility, and be reminded of its *raison d'être*.

Of course, Christians will face dilemmas when the spirit of cooperation clashes with their loyalty to Christ: it would be improper to obey an employer who demands conformity to a policy that is illegal, or the disposal of evidence that would otherwise bring justice to a situation. No employer has the right to ask his staff to lie, break the law or put their lives at risk. However, even at these times of bewilderment, a Christian's obedience and loyalty remain key, and cannot be glibly side-stepped.

Attitude

A Christian employee should have a wholehearted attitude to work (Eph 6:7; Col 3:23), vigorously seeking the success of a business and of all its employees. To such an individual, obedience is not a sullen necessity, borne only out of unavoidable duty, but a lively expression of corporate allegiance. I remember an occasion when members of a group of senior colleagues were asked to donate an hour of their time to support a staffing gap that had arisen in another team. The proposal was greeted with hoots of good-natured derision. However, after a little banter, it became clear that no one was prepared to volunteer. Then one person did. No one followed suit. It was left that other 'volunteers' would be sought after the meeting. When the rota was published later, several people noticed that each gap had been filled by a

Christian. Coincidence? Perhaps. But it illustrates this attitude of wholeheartedness in the face of unappealing chores, of not holding back, of giving when no one else will.

Working wholeheartedly means standing out against making the minimum contribution, clock-watching, rigidly working to rule, and giving the impression of being overworked and underpaid. It means finding no pleasure in refusing to take on other people's burdens. It means avoiding chronic cynicism or self-promotion, and being eager to take reasonable risks, rejoicing in everyone's success. A person with such an attitude is a pleasure to work with.

Thus Christian employees should regard themselves as working in an organisation of which they are thrilled to be part, for a superb Managing Director whom they entirely respect. Their immediate manager may be far from ideal, but they can still continue to work wholeheartedly for him or her out of commitment to the Managing Director. These are not soft words, but a practical challenge that we should be willing to take up.

Expectation

Ultimately there will be a payback time, and then we will see what was good and what was show (1 Cor 3:10–15); but even now, however imperfect, we should expect outstanding work to reap rewards, while misconduct and incompetence receive their just deserts (Eph 6:8; Col 3:24,25). We should expect to succeed when we do well, and to pay a price when we do badly.

Of course, the world is far too perverse a place for that to be the rule. Good work is overlooked, a promised pay rise or honorarium never materializes, or an incompetent colleague is promoted because he or she is politically acceptable. On one occasion I knew of a senior manager who was outraged when a highly competent junior colleague was unjustly ousted in an internal restructuring. Things went from bad to worse for the hapless individual, who was treated as an outcast – deliberately by his foes, and awkwardly by others who intended no harm but had lost their confidence with all the upheaval. Redundancy seemed inevitable after several job applications proved fruitless, despite the manager's best efforts. At the eleventh hour the displaced individual obtained a substantial promotion to another organisation. When the manager was informed, he was heard walking through the corridors shouting, 'Justice! Justice at last!', to the consternation of all around. The aggrieved colleague had been rewarded in line with his manager's proper expectations – even if that reward came from out of the blue!

Nevertheless, when an employee's rightful expectation of reward is denied, he or she should still persevere, trusting in the knowledge that God sees everything. God is the champion of what is right. He will distribute punishment and reward in his good time, either in this life or the next. If 90,000 hours of our life is taken up at work, that we are subjected to injustice for such a high proportion of that time is a matter he takes very seriously. God has no favourites (Eph 6:9; Col 3:25). The Christian at work can look beyond the marketplace to him and be confident that, in the end, justice will prevail. All our actions at work must be based on this assurance.

THE CHRISTIAN EMPLOYER

The two qualities to emerge from Paul's teaching, which can be applied to Christian employers, are a sense of obligation towards employees and an awareness that authority is a privilege given by God which should be used wisely. (Since many people are employees and also supervise or manage other staff on behalf of their employer, they may find that all six qualities mentioned in this chapter apply to them!)

Obligation

The balance of power is heavily weighted in favour of employers, especially if they also own the means of production, so they have a very clear obligation to use that power to provide what is 'right and fair' (Eph 6:9; Col 4:1). Leadership is as much about the moral as the practical, and the Christian employer should be as much 'one who loves what is good, who is self-controlled, upright, holy and disciplined' as a church elder (Titus 1:8): there is no room for one standard for religious leaders but another for business leaders.

Management can portray almost any action as necessary to remain competitive. Often the information needed to judge whether a particular course of action is justified or merely rationalised is not available to the majority of staff in a company. Large pay rises for the top managers – is this genuinely needed to recruit and retain high quality staff in the face of comparable packages on offer from market competitors, or just so much self-indulgence? Redundancies – are they the proper consequence of real investments in productivity, or the simplest way of paying for perks?

The employer holds immense influence over who can or cannot be promoted in an organisation. He or she should constantly be aware that God gives authority for the interests of all, not just the few at the top. Employees naturally expect support, reward, training and development opportunities, encouragement and praise where this is due. It is also incumbent upon an employer to ensure that grievance and disciplinary procedures are fair and consistent, to ensure that all colleagues are pulling their weight and that the organisation's reputation is protected. Every organisation has its share of vested interests, special pleadings and factions with axes to grind. Everyone will see circumstances from their own perspective. A true leader must be prepared to do right even if this puts a lot of people's noses out of joint.

The employer is obliged, both legally and morally, to extend this kind of support to all staff, without favouritism or discrimination. This implies more than instituting a grand policy statement on Equal Opportunities. Favouritism is a form of discrimination that can arise from the subtlest of foundations. It cannot be right for someone's work prospects or conditions to be diminished merely because they belong to some minority group. After all, each of us belongs to some kind of minority or other. Failure to treat all individuals fairly on the basis of their potential is neither fair nor right, and it is the employer's job to combat it.

Privilege

An employee has a huge amount at stake in a job in terms of self-worth and financial security. To lose employment is almost always a disaster for both the individual and his or her dependants. Sometimes an employer may be tempted to use his privileged position, of being able to hire or fire, to intimidate staff: for example, by taking an attitude that says 'like it or lump it'. It may not be said so crudely, but such a attitude can pervade an organisation in countless different ways. It is a dispiriting message, conveying to those concerned that they are not colleagues but disposable assets, not valued but useable, not partners but operatives. Management by threat can infiltrate disciplinary procedures, performance appraisals, business planning, salary reviews and team briefings.

I was once at a meeting in which a director arrived late. When he had gained his bearings, he asked indirectly whether anyone at his level from other departments was expected. When told 'No', he stormed out, muttering. To him, seniority was everything. His high-handed behaviour left us with the strong impression that we should all be more careful of his dignity in the future if we wanted to avoid trouble. Fear can be very effective in galvanising action in the short term, but it is a fast route to contempt and bitterness in the long run.

Employers can also intimidate by exhibiting impatience, rudely interrupting and dismissing the ideas and suggestions of others. They may seek to ease the burden of having to listen, consult and generate support for policies and plans by a variety of petty tyrannies which slap down differences of opinion and frustrate partnership – sidelining a junior colleague, omitting to pass on information, obtaining alternative advice covertly, sitting in uninvited at staff meetings. A popular technique is to create a culture of blame. First, make every effort to ensure that no blame attaches to yourself. Then insist that it was someone else who gave the bad advice. Finally, when everything goes pear-shaped, stir up a witch-hunt (for the benefit of more senior managers), loudly proclaiming that something must be done about those intolerable staff in the Section X, who can never be relied upon to do anything right, even though you have given them very clear instructions. This type of manager is only interested in what he can get out of a job for his own advantage. By losing the respect of his staff in this way, his only recourse is to use intimidation.

In my experience, an effective way to spread blame is to twist the idea of accountability so that someone is held accountable whenever there is a bad result – real or imagined. Nothing is left to chance. Everything is deemed to be due to deliberate acts or omissions, and everyone knows a scapegoat will be found. This is a bully's charter dressed up to look like performance management. If you have encountered one or two 'experts' in this style of management, and have been on the receiving end of their abusive behaviour, remember that God laughs at such tyrants. He promises that, in the end, they will be put to shame and disgraced, their power will vanish and they will be nothing at all (Isa 41:11–13).

Good employers will take great care to avoid using their position of privilege to intimidate. When an armed policeman patrols a street, very few will believe he has no intention of using the large revolver in his holster. The fact of his weapon creates fear; the onus is on him to demonstrate that his intentions are for good, not ill. So it is with the employer. Jesus ridiculed the rulers of his day for lording it over their subjects (Matt 20:25–28): 'whoever wants to be first must be your slave – just as the Son of Man did not come to be served, but to serve,' he said. The leader's real objective should be to serve. Ultimately power can be abused with impunity. Ultimately the only sanction against the corruption of power is the righteous exercise of Higher Power to whom we are all accountable: 'you know that you also have a Master in heaven' (Col 4:1). Ultimately, the Christian employer will face either reward or punishment on the same terms as his employee.

I'll finish with the old joke about the man lost in an air balloon. Bringing it down to twenty feet or so above a field, he asked a man on the ground if he knew where he was.

'In an air balloon twenty feet up,' he replied.

'You must be an engineer,' the balloonist shouted.

'How did you know that?'

'You have just given some accurate information that is completely useless to me.'

'You must be a manager,' said the engineer.

'How did you know that?' rejoined the balloonist.

'Because first of all you're high up. Secondly, you're completely lost and don't know where you're going. And thirdly, now it's all my fault!'

THE CHRISTIAN DISTINCTIVE

Thus we come full circle to the question we asked at the beginning of this chapter – if there is anything distinctive about the Christian at work. In the chapters of Genesis we have looked at so far (Gen 1–3), the whole Godhead – Father and Son and Holy Spirit – is clearly identified with work. In particular, we have noted the difference that the power of the Spirit makes. Indeed, the challenges at work described in the verses from Ephesians and Colossians would be quite beyond us without the help of the Spirit.

Immediately after exhorting his readers about their responsibilities in relation to work, Paul encourages them to 'be strong in the Lord and in his mighty power' (Eph 6:10) and to 'devote yourselves to prayer' (Col 4:2). If we do not seek the power of the Holy Spirit in our work, the raft we are building, to negotiate the rocks on the journey through our working life, will lack power and buoyancy. Most Christians would acknowledge that many of their most authentic answers to prayer concerned work pressures. This is to be expected: the Triune God is at work in our work to fulfil *his* work.

So if there is anything distinctively Christian about our work, it is not that we do certain jobs but that we bring all our occupations to God in prayer: this includes prayer for our colleagues, our performance and the myriad of difficulties that bewilder and beset us. Just as a pastoral minister can be carnal or unconverted, so a bank manager can be prayerful and faithful at work. A dogcatcher or deacon, a blacksmith or a bishop can all rest under the assurance of God's good pleasure if they remain prayerful and faithful in the work to which he has called them.

SUMMARY

Christians are expected to be distinctive in the mundane routines at work because they are called to exhibit qualities that are pleasing to God. These qualities promote harmony and productivity in the workplace. Paul's teaching on work, from Ephesians and Colossians, provides a framework for such harmony, which encompasses:

- an employee's approach to work (with a cooperative spirit);

- an employee's loyalty (to the Lord and thereby to the work);

- an employee's attitude (being wholehearted);

- an employee's expectations (of reward or punishment);

- an employer's obligation (to do what is right);

- an employer's privilege (to shun intimidation).

Promoting harmony at work is not just about boosting efficiency: it is a healthy and vital part of the work situation. It must be rooted in fundamental realities and values, not merely reflected in glossy statements. Its absence is as much a sign of poor working conditions as dangerous machinery.

Christian distinctiveness at work is not just a matter of being predisposed towards certain occupations. Our work, whatever it may be, is an intrinsic part of our duty and calling to follow Christ. We can feel confident, therefore, that secular work is not a second-best calling for the second-rate Christian. Every calling from God has the potential to be fulfilling and creative – God's best for us.

When we take account of what is revealed in Genesis about God the Creator, we are able to understand a little better why it is that he calls so many of his people to ordinary work. We imitate and reflect our Creator in our work, for we are made in the image of a supremely creative God. Work presents enormous opportunities for creativity, service and satisfaction. Undoubtedly, the working world is an arena in which a Christian should learn to exhibit maturity, and we should continually seek to bring work matters to God in prayer.

Pursuing harmony at work is a demanding challenge when so many other agendas seem to take precedence. To achieve harmony will test even the strongest believer. Small wonder, then, that we are expected – in whatever we do, even in the mundane – to work at it with all our heart as working for the Lord.

Chapter 4

PERSEVERANCE

The cutting edge: faith in the furnace

Like a burst boil erupting pus, anger explodes into the working environment; or it oozes gradually into the fabric of an organisation almost unnoticed, concealed by the pressures, tensions and inequalities that remain unresolved, causing untold suffering. I am not aware that any management book exists which attempts to explore anger and suffering at work. It seems that the false divide we set up between our public and private personae leads us to think that to express our real emotions is a sign of weakness, that we should keep a lid on them and confine them to the private, domestic world away from work. However, suppressing our feelings is an unhelpful way of dealing with them. A recent study by the University of Aberdeen suggests that anger is the most commonly suppressed emotion; in particular, its suppression appears to have a disproportionately adverse impact on women who reported feeling more angry, outraged, upset and disgusted than their male counterparts.

In the 90,000 hours making up our working lives, it is highly probable we will encounter times when we feel angry or hurt. These tumultuous, sometimes abject experiences can be defining moments that affect our whole future. There must be few who have not seen businesses forfeited, careers ended, relationships discarded and health broken because of anger and suffering at work.

ANGER

It is not so difficult to understand why a sphere to which human beings give so much of their time can trigger violent eruptions of emotion when people feel diminished or betrayed there. But is it possible, as one person helpfully intimated to me when I was being 'scorched' by the fire of a colleague's wrath, to conduct yourself shrewdly enough to keep out of trouble? Is it only the heavy footed who become entangled in these situations? If the answer to these questions is 'No', how can we survive them? How can we counteract the kind of emotions that the workplace is well able to stir up? Is it right to show anger or to let others know we are hurting? How do we distinguish between different kinds of anger, or express our feelings in ways that do not do lasting damage to others and ourselves? We will start by looking at anger as a right of self-expression.

A right of self-expression

The profusion of advice on assertiveness, self-actualisation and the importance of giving vent to your feelings freely, tends to support the popular view that self-expression is a right. Indeed, the 'stiff upper lip' has been widely discredited as a means of coping with life's problems and is viewed by most people as hypocritical. Anger is more often than not seen as natural and harmless, an emotion which it is unhealthy to restrain. There is evidence that the suppression of powerful emotions can have unpleasant physical and mental symptoms, such as raised blood pressure, depression and listlessness. Some clinical therapy encourages the expression of bottled-up feelings as a step towards healing in a time of crisis. It would seem obvious and right that we should accept the full range of emotions which are, after all, instilled in us by God. Furthermore, it is argued, the Bible is full of examples of righteous anger which as Christians we should follow. If we are seen to be too meek and mild, won't this be inviting others to take advantage of our weakness?

However, what we are considering here is not so much the minor irritations we all encounter daily, but the rather less common, deep inner fury — a kind of overwhelming anger which, for reasons we ourselves rarely understand, creeps up on us and, once stirred up, threatens to engulf us and wreak havoc on our whole lives. I have heard normally rational colleagues descend to the kind of boardroom bellowing that would make a tot's tantrum seem mature. I have read case law in which senior managers have tossed aside a thirty-year career by storming out of an office and into litigation over a malicious remark evidently regarded as the final straw. Anger at work may be the small hinge on which the whole of someone's life can swing in a new and usually adverse direction.

Anger for ill

No one would defend the case for suppressing all forms of anger, as this would be to deny a part of our humanity; however, caution and control seem to be two useful watchwords. Besides presenting us with examples of righteous anger, the Bible also gives a good deal of attention to anger's tendency towards evil. The first example of anger comes early in the Bible (Gen 4:1–12) with the story of Cain and Abel. Cain was filled with resentment because God had received the sacrificial offering of his brother Abel with more favour than his own. God's immediate reaction is one of surprise that Cain should have thought anger was appropriate – 'Why are you angry?' (v 6) – and he warns him, 'if you do not do what is right, sin is crouching at your door…' (v 7). In no time we find that God's misgivings are well founded: Cain's anger leads swiftly to his brother's murder (v 8).

Jonah presents another classic example of misdirected anger. Jonah had just undertaken a major city mission, during which he proclaimed the fearful prospect of God's judgement on the city's inhabitants unless they turned from their evil ways and returned to him. The citizens repented, so God had compassion and 'did not bring upon them the destruction he had threatened' (Jonah 3:10). This infuriated Jonah: 'I knew that you are a gracious and compassionate God… who relents from sending calamity', and he stormed off to sulk outside the city. The Lord provided Jonah with a vine 'to give shade for his head to ease his discomfort, and Jonah was very happy about the vine', Jonah 4:6). But then overnight God caused the vine to wither and the heat of the sun to increase to such an extent that Jonah became even more angry. Not only had God reneged on him and not destroyed the city as promised, he was even depriving Jonah of comfort and shelter. As with Cain, so with Jonah – God asks, 'Have you any right to be angry?' He chides Jonah's concern for the vine in contrast to his indifference to the lives of more than 120,000 people.

The contrast between God's attitude and Jonah's could not be greater. God is gracious and slow to anger: Jonah is judgemental and quick to show petulance and resentment. God treats all people equally: Jonah overlooks his own short-comings (Jonah 1,2) but wants to hold the citizens to account for their sins in spite of their repentance. God is eager to save the city: Jonah is bent on annihilating it. God retains a sense of perspective throughout: Jonah loses all sense of proportion. God's anger is aimed at leading us to our senses and towards forgiveness: human anger all too often leads to self-justification and destruction.

Likewise, in the New Testament, the apostle Paul views anger as giving a foothold to the devil: 'In your anger do not sin. Do not let the sun go down while you are still angry' (Eph 4:26,27). James firmly reminds hotheads consumed by causes and injustices, that despite all appearances to the contrary, anger is seldom a force for God's righteousness (James 1:20). Jesus, echoing the link between anger and murder which we saw in the story of Cain and Abel, drives the point home: 'anyone who is angry with his brother will be subject to judgment' (Matt 5:22).

Anger appears in different forms. On one occasion at work I experienced what I can only describe as overwhelming anger at the increasing workload that was quietly being piled on me as three posts were gradually abolished. This anger was not the red-cheeked, bulbous-eyed variety, but a white heat which churned my deepest feelings for months on end. It surfaced at erratic intervals, often at night, leaving me sleepless. It was uncontrollable – despite my efforts I was powerless to stop it. My mind in turmoil, I endlessly rehearsed imaginary arguments with others about the situation. I suffered indigestion, migraine, exhaustion and depression. I sought medical advice, thinking there must be an organic cause for my deteriorating health – but there was not, and my doctor remained baffled.

At times like these the people around us (apart from close family and friends) are often blissfully unaware of what is happening, not knowing that they are only a hair's breadth away from being struck down with appalling ferocity. Words cannot describe the inner turmoil stoked up by a sense of injustice, powerlessness and longing for vindication. The potential to trample on people's dignity, their self-esteem, their sense of purpose and well-being is enormous. As I saw it, my uncurbed anger would precipitate a worse outcome for myself and for the organisation, so I took my complaints to my line manager – to no effect! When it became clear that there would be no reconsideration of the decision, I was glad to be able to slink away quietly in defeat and pick up meekly where I had left off. After all, others were facing enforced job cuts, and I was probably downplaying real budgetary pressures faced by managers. An expression of overt anger aimed at overthrowing what seems to be an indefensible injustice can frequently turn a problem into a terrible mess – for ourselves, our colleagues, our organisation and our family.

'A fool gives full vent to his anger' (Prov 29:11). Most of us have experienced anger that is used to generate fear and blame. This is particularly despicable when deployed against those over whom you have power. The savage attempt by some managers to unnerve subordinate staff so as to better control them is a form of abuse and unacceptable. It is sickening to see a grown adult emerge from such a tirade shaking and pale. Offenders may try to brush off the seriousness of their action by claiming provocation in the face of a shocking lapse of company standards which cannot be tolerated; they may insist that if so-and-so can't take the heat, she should stay out of the kitchen. But such anger amounts to bullying and degrades the working environment. It may well pump up performance in the short term, but in the long run it will almost certainly inhibit the kind of climate that produces sustained achievement. The perpetrators of such invective are usually unable to control their temper and are behaving like children who cannot get their own way.

When people occupying senior positions feel they cannot get their way, there are usually only two explanations: either they are control freaks who must win on every point, in which case they are unfit for a position of leadership; or they have been promoted into incompetence and need an outlet for their chronic self-doubt. It cost Dame Shirley Porter, former leader of Westminster City Council, some £27 million when she pursued policies that many had apparently tried to warn her were unlawful. The dogged pursuit of a cause at any price can be highly damaging to everyone concerned, including you.

Who should confront a bully if he is very senior? His manager, certainly – promptly and with determination – or he should be confronted by his peers, as the consequences of his behaviour will almost certainly be felt by them. It is not a good idea to leave the victims of his behaviour to try to resolve the problem on their own – they may be the least equipped to cope. Pushed to the extreme, they may suffer a serious decline in performance, health or goodwill towards the organisation.

Confronting and curbing anger at work is not a small matter. To exploit someone's natural fear of failure is distasteful, even cruel, and we should not make excuses for it. I once worked with a senior colleague whose outbursts were so frequent and foul-mouthed that they had a wonderfully comic aspect veering on the entertaining. I justified my non-intervention on the basis that it made him look foolish and no one could take it seriously. In retrospect, I wonder if the staff on the receiving end of their manager's ire could take such a laid-back view. I doubt if my stance was right.

On another occasion a colleague met with me after a meeting I had chaired, to remonstrate with me for failing to rebuke someone who had made a remark at his expense. However, at the time, all concerned – including the butt of the joke – had laughed uproariously. Is there a place for retrospective anger after careful reflection when the heat of the moment is past? This is what my colleague was bringing to me, and I felt I had been put in a no-win situation.

Then there was the staff member who formally asked for an interview with a manager to object to an incident of bullying that involved someone else. However, the manager's bullying was far more widespread. The complainant presented the problem to the manager from several angles, not least the negative impact on the morale of the entire team. Contrary to expectation and after much grumbling, the manager acknowledged the justice of the complaint and made some remarkable improvements. I suspect that this kind of result can only be achieved by prayer and fasting. David, in his psalms, articulated the right approach to dealing with such situations when he wrote: 'In your anger do not sin, when you are on your beds, search your heart and be silent' (Ps 4:4).

Healthy frankness

Most organisations, it seems, would like to deter excessive frankness in the workplace. There may be good reasons for this – ill-judged emotion can have adverse implications for a company's image and commercial confidence. However, many senior managers are adept at the kind of smooth operating that glides glibly over heated issues in the belief that they will go away if ignored. Unfortunately, the reverse is more likely to be true.

The reality is that, under pressure, people experience a natural urge to 'let off steam' and there needs to be room for them to express appropriate levels of anger. Whether we like it or not, anger has an important role to play in allowing the free flow of communication as employees are given the opportunity to exchange information and opinions and be involved in the decisions that affect them. Healthy frankness takes the sting out of difficult situations and opens the way to finding solutions. Disciplinary cases will never develop if those at the receiving end of unacceptable behaviour have means of communicating their frustration firmly but fairly. A healthy frankness is vital for nurturing good relationships and is greatly to be preferred to masked acrimony.

Job displayed such frankness when he gave vent to his feelings about the personal adversity that God had allowed to invade his life. Job was blunt: 'God has unstrung my bow and afflicted me ... He throws me into the mud, and I am reduced to dust and ashes' (Job 30:11,19). He is adamant as to his innocence: 'If I have walked in falsehood or my foot has hurried after deceit – let God weigh me in honest scales and he will know that I am blameless' (31:5,6). Some might regard such language as sacrilegious – indeed, this is the view taken by Job's friends who, in their 'godly' indignation, felt sure Job must have done something wrong for God to permit such adversity (22:4,5; 34:10,11). But God allowed Job's torrent of anger to flow until it was exhausted. When he did finally speak, it was to rebuke Job for his lack of trust rather than his lack of self-control (38–42). Despite his anger, Job retained a correct perspective about God's justice and righteous purposes, unlike his friends.

In Job, God appears to recognise the reality of strong emotion in a fallen human frame and its value when expressed with integrity, so it seems there is a place for anger in the form of healthy frankness. I once became angry with someone from another organisation for being critical about a colleague to our manager and thus tarnishing that person's character. I called the unsuspecting complainant to my office and, to his astonishment, told him what I thought of people who went around damaging the reputations of others. I don't know whether it did him any good, but my colleague was chuffed for days and I certainly felt a whole lot better for it.

Anger for good

It is rare in scripture to find instances when to express anger is viewed as right and proper. For example, when Moses returned from Mount Sinai to see the Israelites revelling in the camp around the golden calf, 'his anger burned' (Exod 32:19,20). Likewise, the prophets were angry about the injustice and financial greed endemic in the society of their day (Isa 10:1,2; Jer 5:26–28; Amos 4:1–3). Phinehas, Aaron's grandson, was permanently rewarded with the priesthood for his uncompromising stance on immorality (Num 25:7–13).

Clearly, since we are made in his image, anger is an emotion given by the Creator to reflect his righteousness and his unhappiness at sin. Its forceful expression in certain circumstances is proper and not invariably to be repudiated. Ironically, however, many people are more inclined to insist on the right to express their anger than to allow God the right to express his. Perhaps we are now ready to contrast God's righteous anger with our own.

God's righteous anger and restraint

Anger is God's response to rebellion. It is evidence of his hostility towards all godlessness and indifference to the truth. In his anger, God may allow us the freedom to indulge in our wickedness and self-destruction (Rom 1:18–25) or he will suddenly intervene (1 Thess 5:3): either way, the consequences are calamitous. Scripture is unequivocal – if we deliberately continue to deny knowledge of the truth, we are left only with a fearful expectation of the raging fire of judgement that will consume the enemies of God. 'It is a dreadful thing to fall into the hands of the living God' (Heb 10:31). His anger is bound up with his holiness which is committed to the destruction of evil and godlessness. One day it will blaze without restraint on all who worship false-hood (Rev 14:9,10). On the other hand, God appears reluctant to unleash his anger: he describes himself to Moses as 'The Lord, the Lord, the compassionate and gracious God, slow to anger and abounding in love and faithfulness' (Exod 34:6). 'For his anger lasts only a moment, but his favour lasts a lifetime' (Ps 30:5).

Jesus reveals God's anger in human form and interestingly reserves some of his most heated criticisms for the established religion of his day. He blazes against religious hypocrisy which exalts self but pollutes others (Matt 23:15), and which values commerce at the expense of ordinary worship (John 2:13–17). Clearly, then, the expression of anger is an authentic aspect of God's personality, but we should remember that we are sinful beings and prone to self-deceit: 'the heart is deceitful above all things and beyond cure. Who can understand it?' (Jer 17:9). It is easy to justify anger in principle but less so in practice. It is easy to fume about perceived injustices, especially when we have heard only one side of the story, and in the workplace it is difficult to be properly informed about everything – the hidden motives, of ourselves and others, will either bamboozle or betray us. Our priority, if we are to honour God, must be to curb these forces without denying them.

However, it is a daunting challenge both to reflect God's anger against injustice while matching his patience and mercy. We cannot hope to succeed if we fail to control the powerful forces of anger. Insofar as we aspire to reflect God's anger, we should strive chiefly to imitate his restraint by being quick to listen and slow to react: 'A man's wisdom gives him patience; it is his glory to overlook an offence' (Prov 19:11).

SUFFERING

We live in a generation that worships hedonism. While there are those who are forced to make difficult choices because of low wages or high housing costs, there are others who choose to live by a formulae for fun. The puzzling phenomenon of prolonged adolescence that this has spawned is amusingly observed in sitcoms such as *Friends* and *Ally McBeal*, as well as in films like *Bridget Jones' Diary*. The inability to delay self-gratification is characteristic of adolescence, and this way of thinking is being extended downwards to ten-year-olds and upwards to age thirty plus. People see no reason to wait for sex, pleasure or purchases. Instead, freed from the shackles of parental and school control, we go our merry way untrammelled, using alcohol to enhance our repartee, available partners for early sexual experimentation, and credit to finance designer gear, leisure and cars. Heavy adult burdens like commitment, marriage, parenting and pension provision are increasingly deferred to the end of thirty-something, to prolong the fun. Serving others in the community is not even a consideration. If living at home sheltered from housing costs and housekeeping chores is the only way to support this lifestyle for a decade or so, then so be it, even if it means sacrificing some degree of independence. Such are 'lovers of pleasure rather than lovers of God' (2 Tim 3:4). By contrast, Paul's words jar on cocooned Western ears:

> [We] rejoice in our sufferings, because we know that suffering produces perseverance; perseverance, character; and character, hope. *Romans 5:3,4*

Perseverance, character, hope – these are three Christ-like qualities that God longs to nurture in each of his children. That they can only be developed through suffering goes against the grain of the prevailing ethos which is hostile to the idea of suffering. We want God to deliver us from our problems, whereas to Paul it is a privilege given to us 'on behalf of Christ not only to believe on him, but also to suffer for him' (Phil 1:29). He was convinced that God set a higher premium on holiness than on happiness, and that suffering has a purpose as part of our calling. It is not an aberration or a sign of failure. It may even be proof of our adoption into God's family (Rom 8:22,23), its absence proof of the contrary.

The strain of suffering

The workplace is studded with the 'walking wounded'. There is the head of a church school suddenly accused of being a child molester; the high flier burned out, to the ill-concealed delight of his colleagues; the candidate embittered by disappointment at not getting a particular job; the malcontent grumbling about his salary grade; the buffoon using bluster to hide his incompetence. There are those who would dearly love to thump their fellow workers, or who feel so undervalued that all creativity and motivation within them has died – only duty and the lack of an alternative keep them at the chalk face. There are the managers who feel locked into the loneliness of listening to others' lies and strategies for self-advancement, or who lock others out from any sense of worth or fulfilment because of their own insatiable ego and greed for profile. With great effort, these people will suppress their feelings of sadness: perhaps it is only another decade or two until retirement.

At times like these, it may seem neither reasonable nor possible to persevere in the weary path of discipleship. Over the years the burden becomes too hard to bear, or something happens which is the straw that breaks the camel's back. Suddenly faith becomes irrelevant, an object of disgust and bitter disappointment. Instead of being a support, it seems as though God redoubles our anguish by refusing to intervene despite our pitiable appeals for help. We feel entangled, overwhelmed, fearful, shaken, rejected, rebuked, forsaken and betrayed. We are unable to wake God or to persuade him to hear our cause. Our enemies pour scorn on our trust in him: to them, our faith seems like an incurable neurosis. They deride us with knowing glances as they whisper behind our backs. A sense of drowning in a torrent of despair may seize us in the middle of the day; the shock of being bludgeoned with clubs may churn our guts in the middle of the night. We are brought down to the dust and there is no relief.

However, we should remember Paul's point that suffering can be constructive or destructive, depending on our attitude. Although suffering may seem alien to our natural thoughts and inclinations, there are aspects of God and his nature which may only be known through suffering. Far from abandoning their faith, many come to faith for the first time through such experiences.

> For it is commendable if a man bears up under the pain of unjust suffering because he is conscious of God. But how is it to your credit if you receive a beating for doing wrong and endure it? But if you suffer for doing good and you endure it, this is commendable before God. To this you were called, because Christ suffered for you, leaving you an example, that you should follow in his steps.
>
> 'He committed no sin,
>   and no deceit was found in his mouth.'
>
> When they hurled their insults at him, he did not retaliate; when he suffered, he made no threats. Instead, he entrusted himself to him who judges justly. He himself bore our sins in his body on the tree, so that we might die to sins and live for righteousness; by his wounds you have been healed. For you were like sheep going astray, but now you have returned to the Shepherd and Overseer of your souls.   *1 Peter 2:19–25*

This passage on suffering comes immediately after Peter's teaching on submission to those in authority both in government and at work (1 Pet 2:13–18). Here he argues that followers of Christ must expect to suffer unjustly. This is something quite different from facing the just consequences of our actions, which is, in effect, deserved suffering. By contrast, the emphasis here is on patience rather than justice; following Christ's example rather than accepting God's righteous punishment; the privilege of receiving God's commendation rather than the repercussions resulting from disobedience.

Peter is envisaging a situation where the rough and tumble of the workplace provides a Christian with the context for doing good. Our spiritual growth and maturing do not take place only in the hallowed aisles of the church building, but also in the spit and bile of the marketplace. The crises we face at work, or anywhere else, are not the tributaries to our spiritual life but the mainstream. It is in them that God himself is seen at work, shaping and purifying our souls through what may seem to us to be incidental.

A W Tozer speaks of God's work in our lives at these times as being designed to take away the veil that hides his face from us, which only he can remove. This metaphor of the veil may seem 'poetical, almost pleasant', but Tozer adds:

> In actuality there is nothing pleasant about it. In human experience that veil is made of living human tissue; it is composed of the sentient quivering stuff of which our whole beings consist, and to touch it is to touch us where we feel pain. To tear it away is to injure us, to hurt us and make us bleed. To rip through the dear and tender stuff of which life is made can never be anything but deeply painful.

Suffering may take different forms – gratuitous bullying, the thoughtless indifference of a normally considerate manager enduring pressures of her own, or the arrogance of corrupted power that says, 'It is your job to do as I say.' (Some Christian organisations may present the latter as a biblical requirement.

Although Christian leadership is meant to be fundamentally about serving, some heavy-handed leaders still clobber their flock with high sounding nonsense designed to inflate their own importance.) Months or years of loyal service are forgotten overnight. Achievements from last year's hours of unpaid overtime become a screaming irrelevance as new realities emerge.

Taking tough action may seem the only way out and the boss does not flinch. Is there a need for a scapegoat to blame for past mistakes, quick savings in staff overheads, new levels of output from the same team which has already doubled output in the last three years? Is there a need for a new organisational structure that owes more to erasing the legacy of a predecessor than to shaping the conditions for future success? Is this a good time to promote 'one of us' and hamstring 'one of them'? Is this an opportunity to humiliate 'disloyal' colleagues who won't toe the line? Whatever is needed must be implemented *now*. Loyalty is measured by the capacity to say the word 'yes'.

Harsh times may also be just the way things are – awkward, fortuitous, unfair, impenetrably complex, a product of other people's carelessness or honest mistakes. The more senior you become, the more you are expected to generate solutions. One of the greatest pressures on a manger is the urge to act decisively, to clear away the creeping vines and show you are in control. A fuller understanding of the picture may indicate that it would be folly to act just yet, but this just looks like a failure of resolve. Premature action may hack to pieces options as well as obstacles. Good timing requires great determination.

What can Christians do under such circumstances, particularly when it impinges on themselves, their colleagues or their staff? Is meek silence an adequate response? Should we make use of formal grievance procedures or litigation, which may only make matters worse or divert attention away from more urgent problems threatening the business? Does it make a difference if injustice affects only us and not others? How should we respond when work problems seem to staple us to the floor? What are we to make of our emotions in the face of confident pronouncements in the Bible such as 'nothing will be able to separate us from the love of God' (Rom 8:39)? Who has not tasted brief periods of what Brian Keenan, during his time as a Beirut hostage, called 'crucifying aloneness. There's a silent, screaming slide into the bowels of ultimate despair.' Should we do what seems sincerely right in our own eyes and take matters into our own hands, sure that God would not have us suffer so? The temptation to escape stress may be overwhelming at the point of breakdown.

Some years ago I faced many months with little to do at work, marooned in a backwater under subtle probing as to where I saw my future. Many voices urged me to do something, if only to end the humiliation: simply wallowing around doing nothing was to set myself up as an easy target. However, I clung to these words from Isaiah:

> Let him who walks in dark,
>   who has no light,
> trust in the name of the Lord
>   and rely on his God.
> But now, all you who light fires
>   and provide yourselves with flaming torches,
> go, walk in the light of your fires
>   and of the torches you have set ablaze.
> This is what you shall receive from my hand:
>   You will lie down in torment.   *Isaiah 50:10,11*

The strain of suffering may tempt us to give way, but then everything we could gain from it would also be washed away, and we would be left with nothing of real and long-lasting value.

Responses to suffering

The verses from Peter do not offer simple answers to suffering. Where we might expect a strong line in assertiveness, collective action, frank confrontation and threats of resignation, he suggests other principles we should keep in mind when determining how to respond to suffering.

Respect those in authority (1 Peter 2:13–18)

First, we are enjoined to respect (v 17, translated as 'fear' from the Greek) our managers by virtue of their office, and to submit to (v 18, 'remain under') them, irrespective of how unworthy they may be of our support.

What does this respect and submission look like in practice? Is it servile and sullen? Is it to demean the staff member and inflate the manager? No – biblical submission is given to human society by the only wise God to protect and support the heavy office of leader, while at the same time preserving the dignity and security of those who are being led. Every bloody revolutionary, terrorist and boardroom rebel has alleged that they love only justice and peace, and that they are driven to overthrow authority only because of that authority's abuse of power. But the office of power is a safeguard against potentially worse injustice. Every leader faces demanding and conflicting pressures with some degree of bias, weakness and self-interest. Every leader must eventually deal with personal shortcomings. The wise leader will not treat these as setbacks but as personal opportunities to change.

As a young man, I once had a chance encounter with my august director in the gents (the only place I was ever likely to meet him personally)! He had heard that I had been unsuccessful in a recent job application. Facing the urinal, he made some polite remarks, then added conspiratorially, 'You would not believe me if I told you how many job interviews

I failed in my career.' I wondered what lay behind this unguarded and kindly admission from a man viewed in his time as an exceptional high flier. He had persevered and remained free of bitterness. Many do not.

It is easy to believe that replacing someone in authority with someone else would be beneficial. In biblical thinking, to refuse to submit to authority is only justified when that authority commands direct disobedience to God (Acts 5:27–32), but this cannot be made into the loophole that takes in every disaffection. God has appointed every human authority, both good and evil, for purposes only he can explain. Enduring the behaviour of your manager may be his purpose for you. However, be assured that your manager also bears a heavy responsibility before God in exercising authority over you.

A powerful leader in his day, David lived with a multiplicity of threats – personal, social, military and political. Many ambitious and unscrupulous contenders were just waiting to see the king drop his vigilance. Even the most efficient secret service could not be alert to intrigue night after night, year after year. Assassination in those days was commonplace, and eunuchs patrolling the royal bedchamber were sometimes cheap to bribe. In Psalm 25, David reflects on the source of his help as the nation's chief justice, field marshal and supreme governor. Who could he truly rely on to free him from trouble and anguish? Who would shelter him from the heat and chill of baffling government responsibilities? Who would be equal to the exhausting task of vigilance in the face of endless snares?

> To you, O Lord, I lift up my soul;
>   in you I trust, O my God.
> Do not let me be put to shame,
>   nor let my enemies triumph over me…
> Guard my life and rescue me;

> let me not be put to shame,
> for I take refuge in you. *Psalm 25:1,2,20*

So, while it may be tempting, we should try to avoid joining in ubiquitous backchat against managers and generally undermining them. No leader is capable of carrying out his or her responsibilities properly without help and advice from colleagues. We can support them by taking our own responsibilities seriously, performing them well and whole-heartedly, and participating fully in the workplace. Perhaps this will involve pointing out the flaws or dangers in a proposed action, or actively contributing to the discussion leading up to important decisions. It takes grit to continue giving conscientious advice when it is repeatedly discarded as unwelcome. But by doing our best at work, we will achieve dignity and security as servants of Christ.

I have been very fortunate with the ten or so managers I have worked for. With rare exception, I have felt able, even privileged, to learn from their gifts and experience. They have supported and encouraged me in my progress and development. They have given me many opportunities for formal training and special assignments. They have shared any success with me.

The exception burdened me with indescribable stress that drained me of morale and motivation. Coming to work to be undermined and marginalised was a daily effort. Others would come to me to unload their own resentments and compare notes. While these moments offered some relief, in the long run such dubious support only increased my sense of impotence. If this is happening to you, giving respect to your manager may seem like applying ice cream to a sensitive tooth. But keep in mind that God has purposes in suffering, and he may be using that person to develop your character in ways you can only now imagine.

Endure suffering patiently (1 Peter 2:19–23)

It is important when thinking about this second principle to ensure that we are especially aware of our dependence on God, and are not washed away by feelings of abandon and chance. In the end, God is our anchor – he sees, he understands and he will judge righteously in his own time. This is not at all the same as saying that we should leave it solely to him to find the solutions to all our problems. His purpose more often than not is simply to help us endure to the end without breaking down or taking refuge in retaliation. Our endurance brings God pleasure in that it is evidence that the image of Christ is thus being distinctively formed in his children.

To follow the example of Christ, who endured suffering patiently, is part of our calling, however unappealing it may seem. We profess to be his disciples but we are not always keen to follow in his footsteps. But if we do, it is 'commendable' (v 19, Greek *charis*) – a rich word, implying purpose rather than accident, suggesting that to endure suffering is a favour, a gift, a pleasure and a gracious commission from God. Paul describes the office of apostle in this way: 'Through him and for his name's sake, we received grace and apostleship to call people from among all the Gentiles to the obedience that comes from faith' (Rom 1:5). It is the privilege of all followers of Christ to suffer in their work. That joy may bubble up in the midst of suffering is an experience attested to by Paul and Silas in their stocks in the Philippian jail (Acts 16:22–25) but it cannot obscure the fact that these times may also seem like going through fire.

God has a way of testing us at our weakest point, which is usually our strongest point of challenge to God's priority over our lives. We can see this happening in the life of Abraham, who was tested over God's promise that he would have a great nation of descendants through a son by his childless wife, Sarah (Gen 12:2; 15:4,5; 17:2). However, as life went on and nothing seemed to be going the way God promised, Abraham and Sarah thought they could manoeuvre the situation into bringing the promise about. So Abraham agreed to Sarah's suggestion that he sleep with her servant, Hagar, to obtain a child and heir (16:1–4). It turns out to be the wrong decision: Sarah became jealous and treated Hagar badly, forcing her to run away. Then later, when Isaac was born as God promised, the antagonism between the two boys and their mothers increased. Abraham failed that test with flying colours.

However, some years later, Abraham received a clear command from God that he must sacrifice Isaac (22:2–18). The narrative of Abraham's extended anguish is unbearable: one can picture the innocent boy with the timber on his back, eagerly prancing alongside his distraught father, not knowing where he was going and why. Only at the eleventh hour, when Abraham had nearly drunk from the cup of horror, does God provide a substitute sacrifice in the form of a ram. This test of faith Abraham passed with flying colours. Over the year, his faith in God had grown to such an extent, he was willing to take obedience to the limit.

Was God playing with Abraham's feelings? Was it a case of deliberate cruelty? A test to teach Abraham a lesson on the nature of faith (22:12)? Perhaps. But this incident also has wider consequences both for Abraham and for us, foreshadowing the coming of Jesus through Abraham's descendants from Isaac, and the suffering that God himself would undergo as he watched his Son die on the cross at Calvary. No last-minute intervention then.

To many, the blood sacrifice demanded of Abraham seems primitive and unnecessarily violent. This is a theme in Girish Karnad's bold and vigorous play, *Bali – The Sacrifice*, inspired by a Jain epic poem written in AD 959. A mahout (elephant handler) of the king has a singing voice that has drawn many women to his bed, where his skills apparently match his crescendo. This night his passionate lovemaking, described in vivid, scratching intensity, turns out to have been with the queen. Her husband, noticing her absence from the royal bed, follows her to the temple chamber where he discovers what has happened. Despite his Jain commitment to non-violence, the king can barely restrain himself from driving his sword through his servant. The queen mother, resentful of her son's conversion to his wife's bloodless Jain faith, goads him to kill his wife, offer the gods a blood sacrifice or do something, instead of whining impotently about how much he wants her back. The queen protests her innocence based on her lack of intent ('It just happened ... it won't happen again').

So the grand themes are set on a collision course – casual sex, betrayal, adultery, an interfering mother-in-law, sin, grace, forgiveness, sacrifice, restoration. The central question is, what price does it cost to cleanse away a profound wrong and be released from its stain? In the Bible, Abel answered with a blood sacrifice and his brother Cain a bloodless one. God's favour towards Abel led Cain, the bloodless one, to bloody fratricide. In *Bali*, resolution comes when the queen, driven to the limit by her struggle to prevent her husband from offering a blood sacrifice, finally turns the knife on herself.

We should expect at some stage in our lives to be tested in our work. Perhaps this will be at the point of ambition, redundancy, personal dispute or failure. Equally, those who have chosen to make the home their main work arena may be tested by problems arising out of the loss of a secure income, social status or community due to relocation of the job of their employed partner. How can we come through the test, remaining faithful to our calling to Christian discipleship? Perhaps it is by being forced to stop trusting in our own skills and relying on our own understanding. Instead, if we wait for God to judge rightly in our situation, he promises to rescue us from deep water, to bring peace and to sustain us in trouble. He will reveal the justice of our cause and prevent our condemnation at trial. He holds victory in store for the upright. We may sometimes be tempted to doubt all this, but it remains true. Our reassurance comes from our Shepherd in whom we trust.

Trust Christ, 'the Shepherd and Overseer of your souls' (1 Peter 2:23–25)

For many Christians, the anguish is at its most piercing when God seems to turn away in silent disinterest. We may find our distress at this difficult to share with others: we may risk being regarded as a joke by those who have not experienced the profound love that God shows us through his tender involvement in the daily details of our life and work. When God's throne-room seems shut for business, it may be difficult to get guidance from elsewhere, even from other Christians who often take the view that God's deafness to our prayers must be the result of our waywardness and therefore our fault. As we have seen, Job's friends were experts on this subject. But suffering is a poor guide as to whether or not we are in God's favour, and feeling depressed is not a sign that we are outside of God's will. We need to keep telling ourselves this fact, as we may find it difficult to believe when submerged by doubts.

To make matters worse, out of the 'dark night of the soul' tantalising glimpses of hope may beckon. Many months into a 'shut for business' period, as I was reading a psalm one night, a particular verse seemed to leap off the page – 'joy comes in the morning' (Ps 30:5). At around four morning, I was awakened by a vivid dream involving a clear view of a signpost with the name of a town legible on it. Later that morning, my boss called me in to say that he had met a colleague from this same town, who had announced his retirement. My boss suggested I should apply for his job.

I was thunderstruck. Nothing happened for three months, then the advertisement appeared. I applied; I was called for interview; I was unceremoniously rejected. I was confused and disappointed.

Five years later, I was praying about another vacant post. Shortly before the closing date for sending in an application, I was sitting in a darkened auditorium at a conference, when a latecomer clambered into the seat next to me. When the lights went up, I saw it was the person presently in the post I was considering. We had a very useful briefing discussion in the coffee interval. Then the next day, as I was leaving the auditorium for coffee, I bumped into the recruitment consultant handling the application process, who was unexpectedly visiting the conference for the day. We had another very useful briefing discussion in another coffee interval! I applied for the post; I was called for interview; I was unceremoniously rejected. I was confused and disappointed.

How can we make sense of this? Perhaps it was not so much a case of external direction but internal discovery. The most uncontroversial advice I received about both these incidents was from a friend who told me God had wanted me to apply for both jobs and had also wanted me to fail to get them. Abraham was clearly guided by God to sacrifice his only son, Isaac, but in trusting God and setting out to obey him, that guidance changed. Depending on God, and on God alone, is a test from which none of us emerges unscathed or unchanged. The battle we face revolves around whether we really believe that he wants the best for us and can be trusted, or whether we don't. The choice is unavoidable – it is an aspect of the heavenly conflict between good and evil. Our banal circumstances and seemingly petty worries are in fact the cudgels picked up by unseen powers to defeat our faith.

Suffering was a regular feature of David's life, and he reflects this dichotomy in his psalms. In Psalm 22, he cries,

'My God, my God, why have you forsaken me?' Yet in Psalm 23, he asserts, 'The Lord is my Shepherd, I shall not want...' David sees no contradiction in believing both perspectives: the times when God appears to be absent and the times when he is constantly near seem to him a normal part of life. We, too, need to accept both, with the patient realism that the one will in due course give way to the other as night follows day. In her book Affliction, Edith Schaeffer depicts two rectangles. One contains all the conquests we have won, which we can describe as victories. The other contains all the trials we have endured, which are just as significant victories. The one is a test of courage, the other a test of patience. Both are tests of faith.

Although for now he may seem 'all-silent' in the presence of our suffering, and our prayers appear to make no difference, God is all-powerful, all-loving and all-knowing, a fact we need constantly to remind ourselves:

> O Lord, you have searched me
> and you know me.
> You know when I sit and when I rise;
> you perceive my thoughts from afar.
> You discern my going out and my lying down;
> you are familiar with all my ways...
> You hem me in – behind and before;
> you have laid your hand upon me...
> All the days ordained for me
> were written in your book
> before one of them came to be...
> See if there is any offensive way in me,
> and lead me in the way everlasting. *Psalm 139:1–3,5,16,24*

...the Lord delights in those who fear him, who put their hope in his unfailing love. *Psalm 147:11*

So, do we turn away from the faith, and 'curse God and die'

(Job 2:9)? Or do we entrust ourselves in our suffering to him who alone judges rightly? It is in making the right decision that we demonstrate our trust in the Christ, 'the Shepherd and Overseer of our souls'. He is our example in that he suffered but also entrusted himself to God. In him, we see the power of God at work, sustaining faith under pressure despite all evidence to the contrary. In him, we see the fruit of maturing faith – perseverance, character and an unshakable 'hope of the glory of God' (Rom 5:2)

Christ's death on the cross lies at the heart of biblical faith. By carrying our sins in his body on the cross, he provides us with three truths we can draw on to sustain us during our toughest times:

- **No injustice at work will go unjudged**. Sin was punished on the cross in the body of one who had committed no sin. We can be reassured, therefore, that some day he will judge every wrongdoing inflicted upon us, and this reassurance will give us the power to let go of all resentment and the words of anger leading to discouragement that replay in our minds.

- **Selfish passion can be combated by a passion for what is right**. Christ's death heralded the death of sin, terminally wounding sin's power over us and opening up the possibility of a life committed to doing what is right. Pragmatic cynicism need not have an irresistible hold on us; we do not have to bow to prevailing opinion, dismiss reforms as unworkable, or assume that money and self are the only motivators for people at work. We don't need to surrender to the ways of the world, however feeble we may feel. Righteousness can flourish amidst cynicism.

- **Christ has taken upon himself the worst consequence of our sin, namely our separation from God.** You and I deserve to suffer the fall-out of sin as we endure the individual and collective outcomes of our fallen human nature. Pain and suffering, malice and meanness, disappointment and distress – these are occupational hazards – but never destitution and hopelessness. While we were utterly alienated from God, debarred from access to the light of his presence, Jesus Christ voluntarily took our place and our punishment upon himself. Now we will never be God-forsaken. There can be hope amidst hardship.

Patience amidst injustice, righteousness amidst cynicism, and hope amidst hardship. These may sound like rhetorical ideals, and they will remain so unless sound theological realities exist to substantiate them. The death of Christ is the reality. The mystery of Christ's death on the cross in our place, so clearly taught in Scripture, provides a future hope rooted in certainty which while unseen is more concrete than anything we see on earth: 'But hope that is seen is no hope at all. Who hopes for what he already has? But if we hope for what we do not yet have, we wait for it patiently' (Rom 8:24–25).

Our hope is that we will one day return to 'the Shepherd and Overseer of our souls' who alone knows how to look after our deepest needs. He will care for us all our lives and manage us when we would sink. He intends to carry out this pastoral support and personal development during the 90,000 hours we spend at work as much as anywhere else. He is at work with us and in us, and if we trust in him, who knows what our work will achieve?

> Why are you downcast, O my soul?
> Why so disturbed within me?

Put your hope in God,
for I will yet praise him,
my Saviour and my God.   *Psalm 42:11*

SUMMARY

Anger is a mixed blessing – it can be ludicrous or it can be destructive. It is far more pervasive in the workplace than we generally acknowledge. There is a place for frank expression of opinion, and anger sometimes needs to be expressed in a limited number of circumstances, usually associated with injustice. By contrast, God's righteous anger sets standards that humans cannot easily attain, and provides a distinction between God and humankind. A profound challenge for us is to imitate God's restraint in curbing our natural tendency to lose our temper, knowing that God is slow to anger while we are quick to self-justify. God's anger brings righteousness; human anger often does not. We find the right balance when we express God's righteous anger with his restraint and forbearance.

Suffering is a universal human experience which cannot be evaded by meticulous obedience and clever choices. In the workplace, it may be part of God's purpose in shaping and developing a Christian. These 'fiery trials' are intended to leave us burnished as pure gold (1 Pet 1:6–7), not burned out like old cars. Like the three civil servants thrown into the fiery furnace for refusing to worship the politically correct image of their day (Dan 3:17–18, 27), we should expect to go through blazing heat. We know that God can preserve us without our being singed by the flames, if he chooses to do so. The world does not believe that Christian faith can withstand harsh provocation in the marketplace. Foolish people talk ignorantly about Christians to bring their faith into disrepute, but faithful discipleship under suffering can silence detractors as effectively as any argument. Suffering is part of God's plan, not some ghastly accident. We are urged to persevere in the face of unjust suffering with our mind set on three attitudes:

- respect authority submissively, especially authority that is exercised over us;
- endure suffering patiently, with all its attendant heartaches and joys; and
- trust Christ faithfully as he shepherds and oversees us through the creative anguish that is our calling.

These are the qualities that we, as Jesus' flock, need to demonstrate in a working life that can take up 90,000 hours of our life, patiently enduring the perplexing and often painful pressures that come our way. Only then will we see Christian maturity take root. For our Shepherd leads us along paths that show us that 'suffering produces perseverance; perseverance, character; and character, hope. And hope does not disappoint us' (Rom 5:3–5).

Conclusion

WORKING FOR CHRIST

90,000. This is an enormous number of hours in any life to give to work, paid or unpaid. As we have progressed through the chapters of this book, we have explored many issues connected with work, and have noted the distinctive contributions made by Scripture, through which God speaks afresh to every generation.

In first three chapters of Genesis, we discovered the Creator God at work. Creativity is the foundation of work; indeed, creativity is work as God intended. He created human beings in his image and as such we reflect his creativity. Using our creativity is our only way forward in finding solutions to the welter of personal and global problems that beset us, such as poverty, disease, unequal income distribution, environmental destruction and all the other consequences of human sin.

God invites men and women to reflect his creativity by enjoying and sustaining his creation. We are liberated to do this within the framework of his moral qualities by being rational, righteous, responsible, restful and relational, reflecting in particular the unselfish and loving relationship demonstrated by the Trinity – Father, Son and Holy Spirit. Work offers us the opportunity to put this framework into action – to love, be creative, achieve fulfilment, serve others and be productive. However, human beings have made the deliberate choice to live apart from God. This self-determination brings disaster in the shape of God's righteous judgement upon us. As a result, conflict, pain and alienation become an established part of work as we experience it now, after the fall.

Having rejected the option of being God-centred, we slowly discover that the only other option is to live in a world that is self-centred. We can serve God's economy, or we can serve humanity's economy. Overworked and underplayed we become beset by the stresses and strains that pockmark our lives. Workaholism and unemployment coexist in the form of two-income households and no-income households. Boredom and breaking point coexist in the same organisation. Overvalued careers become an unsatisfying grind. People who feel undervalued become unmanageable. Creativity coexists with crisis.

As we seek to awaken a biblical pulse in our working life, we encounter demands more rigorous than work itself. We are expected to approach work with the spirit of cooperation, to owe unyielding loyalty to the Lord amidst arrogance that scorns our faith. We are called to serve our work colleagues wholeheartedly and conscientiously. Through good times and bad, however, we can be assured that right behaviour will receive its just reward and unrighteous behaviour its just punishment. None of this is achievable without constant turning to prayer, unafraid to bring every working issue, major and minor, to the throne of God. Our calling has the importance of being his calling, and no calling is more important than that. In such circumstances, we may find ourselves in a state of inner turmoil as we encounter frustration in a world that is not centred on us, and realise that our needs and desires probably won't be fulfilled as we might wish. Managing a range of expressions of anger is a bit like controlling and breaking a horse – although often it may seem that we are not so much horse whisperers as 'hoarse' whisperers!

Then there is the waiting: 'How long, O Lord? Will you forget me for ever?' (Ps 13:1). Fiery trials and psychological suffering, of which others may be oblivious, can be inflicted on us at work maliciously and without provocation. Our own folly or inexperience may bring us problems. Maintaining submissive respect to proper authority over us, while persevering through times of personal darkness, produces a rare quality of patience, character and hope. But at what price? The choice is stark: we can trust Christ to be the competent Shepherd of our souls; or we can look to ourselves to light our own fires and ignite a self-made destiny far away from God's hidden purposes:

> Now all has been heard;
>> here is the conclusion of the matter:
> Fear God and keep his commandments,
>> for this is the whole duty of man. *Ecclesiastes 12:13*

In all this, we have set before us some of the valuable things Scripture has to say about work. Scripture is intensely practical in helping us to find ways of coping with the challenges and possibilities of working life in a broken world. Fellow travellers may be encouraged to begin addressing for themselves the myriad issues that arise uniquely for Christians in all the different enterprises – public, private and voluntary – in which they participate. New materials and new themes may emerge, to be developed and applied in different arenas. A radical new encyclopaedia of contemporary Christian thinking on work is waiting to be written.

God has assigned to us work that is unique to each of us as individuals. At times, we may elevate that work as an end in itself and worship the gift rather than the Giver. At other times, we may find it hard to discern the assignment at all, viewing it as more a matter of chance than a deliberate commission. We may even devalue our work, regarding it as of little worth, embarrassed that it could even be described as God's work for us. In all these ways, we can end up obstructing the Creator God in accomplishing his work of saving and renewing his creation.

Four basic themes resonate throughout Scripture and offer us a way of finding a route through the rocks and rapids of our working life: creativity, rest, harmony and perseverance. These themes present us with insights and approaches to our work which, individually and corporately, we can make concrete in the vast array of activities God has prepared for us to do. If we commit ourselves to building creativity, rest, harmony and perseverance into every aspect of our work, we will recover some degree of order, purpose and meaning in our world. Then we will cease to keep God out of something that takes up so much of each day of our lives, and we will have made some progress towards reconciling the Bible and public life. In unleashing God's Word, we will find that wisdom is increasingly to be found in the marketplace. We may discover that we are in fact collaborating with God in all kinds of ways and for purposes we could scarcely have imagined. And finally, we will discover, to our intense delight, that we have been occupying a royal position – working all along in the service of Christ.

BIBLIOGRAPHY

Agrell, Goran, *Work, Toil and Sustenance*, Verbum, 1976.

Baldwin, Stanley, *Take this Job and Love it*, InterVarsity Press, 1988.

Banks, Robert, *God the Worker*, Albatross Books, 1992.

Banks, Robert, *All the Business of Life*, Albatross Books, 1987.

Banks, Robert (ed), *Private Values and Public Policy*, Lancer, 1983.

Banks, Robert, *The Tyranny of Time*, InterVarsity Press, 1983.

Beasley-Murray, Paul, *Dynamic Leadership*, MARC Europe, 1990.

Biggar, Nigel, *Good Life*, SPCK, 1997.

Blanchard, Kenneth and Johnson, Spencer, *The One-Minute Manager*, Fontana, 1983.

Blocher, Henri, *In the Beginning: The opening chapters of Genesis*, InterVarsity Press, 1984.

Calvin, John, *Institutes of the Christian Religion*, Macdonald, nd.

Cormack, David, *Team Spirit: People working with people*, MARC Europe, 1987.

De Vaux, Roland, *Ancient Israel*, Dartman, Longman and Todd, 1973.

Greene, Mark, *Thank God it's Monday*, Scripture Union, 1994, 2001.

Harvey-Jones, John and Masey, Anthea, *Troubleshooter*, BBC Books, 1990.

Helm, Paul, *The Callings*, Banner of Truth, 1987.

Higginson, Richard, *Transforming Leadership*, SPCK, 1996.

Houston, James, *I Believe in the Creator*, Hodder and Stoughton, 1979.

John Paul II, *Laborem Exercens*, The Papal Encyclical on Human Work, Catholic Truth Society, 1984.

Kakabadse, Andrew, Ludlow, Ron and Vinnicombe, Susan, *Working in Organisations*, Penguin Business, 1988.

Kidner, Derek, *Wisdom to Live By*, InterVarsity Press, 1985.

Lewis, C S, *Fern-seed and Elephants, and other essays on Christianity*, Fontana, 1975.

Lewis, C S, *Christian Reflections*, Eerdmans, 1967.

Lucas, R C, *Fullness and Freedom: The Message of Colossians and Philemon*, InterVarsity Press, 1980.

Quirk, Barry, *Esprit de Corps: Leadership for progressive change in local government*, Joseph Rowntree Foundation, 2001.

Richardson, Alan, *The Biblical Doctrine of Work*, SCM Press, 1952.

Rush, Myron D, *Management: a Biblical Approach*, Victor Books, 1983.

Ryken, Leland, *Work and Leisure in Christian Perspective*, Multnomah Press, 1987.

Sayers, Dorothy L, *Creed or Chaos?*, Methuen, 1947.

Schaeffer, Edith, *Affliction*, Baker Book House, 1993.

Schaeffer, Francis, *The Letters of Francis Schaeffer*, Kingsway, 1986.

Schumacher, Christian, *To Live and Work*, MARC Europe, 1987.

Sherman, Doug and Hendricks, William, *Your Work Matters to God*, NavPress, 1987.

Stott, John, *Issues Facing Christians Today*, Marshalls, 1984.

Tozer, A W, *The Pursuit of God*, Christian Publications, 1995.

Westcott, David, *Work Well: Live Well*, Marshall Pickering, 1996.

Other Resources
from Scripture Union

Thank God it's Monday
Ministry in the Workplace

Mark Greene

ISBN: 1 85999 208 0, £5.99

Fun, fast, and full of stories, this highly practical book looks at how we can make the most of the time we spend at work. This updated and expanded edition includes a new chapter on the ethical challenges that face us. A revised resource section further reinforces the already strong position of Mark Greene's book in the marketplace.

B format, 180pp

Christian Life and Work package
(Video editor: Rob Purbrick)

ISBN 1 85999 532 2

A six-part 2 hour video keyed into Mark Greene's book Thank God it's Monday. Includes a leader's guide and a copy of the book. Topics include, 'Introducing a Theology of Work', 'Evangelism in the Workplace', 'Relating to the Boss', 'Truthtelling and Handling Pressure at Work', and 'Work & Spirituality'. Presenters: Mark Greene and others.

A format pb 192pp + workbook 60pp + video £25.00

Christian Life and Today's World package
(Video editor: Rob Purbrick)

ISBN 1 85999 576 4

How can we take up the challenge of living as Christians in a postmodern society? From SU and LBC comes another stimulating small group resource containing video, accompanying workbook for group leaders and book of articles written by members of the LBC faculty.

A format pb 192pp + workbook 60pp + video £25.00

Wake up to Work

Geoff Shattock

ISBN: 1 85999 309 5, **£2.99**

Bite-sized reflections on issues relating to taking faith to work. True life stories and clear teaching make this an easy and encouraging read.

Light from a Dark Star
Where's God when my world falls apart?

Wayne Kirkland

ISBN: 1 85999 515 2, **£4.99**

It's the big question that won't go away. Why does God allow suffering? There are no simple answers in this book. No attempts to shrug off the serious challenges to faith which the question raises. Rather it engages compassionately with the sufferings of real people, grappling with slippery issues, in a discovery of some intriguing perspectives.

Knowing God's Ways

A user's guide to the Old Testament

Patton Taylor

ISBN: 1 85999 349 4, **£6.99**

Do you find the Old Testament difficult to get into? If you've been looking for some help in making sense of it all, then this book by a professor at Union Theological College in Belfast is what you've been looking for! His accessible. user-friendly approach will help you gain a clear overview of the Old Testament, understand different genres, and apply biblical teaching to today's world.

Journey into the Bible

John Drane

ISBN: 1 85999 409 1, **£4.99**

In his usual thought-provoking and accessible style John Drane gives a stimulating introduction to many of the issues raised by reading the Bible today. Designed especially for those who are struggling to come to terms with the Bible.

Dangerous Praying

Inspirational Ideas for individuals and groups

David Spriggs

ISBN: 1 85999335 4, **£6.99**

Drawing on Paul's letter to the Ephesians, this creative book challenges us to be bold when we pray, both in what we pray for and how we pray. David Spriggs presents us with 101 practical ideas and strategies to help us develop a courageous prayer life, whether in a group or individually.

Faith and Common Sense
Living boldly, choosing wisely

David Dewey

ISBN: 1 85999 302 8, **£4.99**

This unusual book explores how we can live riskily yet sensibly. Drawing on the lives of key Bible characters like Peter, the author first lays a solid biblical and theological foundation for achieving a balance. Then follows a practical look at areas in our lives where a need for that balance is vital - healing, the gifts of the Spirit, work, money, failure and guidance.

The Bible Unwrapped
Developing your Bible skills

David Dewey

ISBN: 1 85999 533 0, **£5.99**

Is the Bible something of a closed book to you? Here you'll find help in finding your way around the Bible, and in grasping the big picture of the Bible's message. You'll also learn to appreciate the different types of literature in the Bible and be introduced to eight different approaches to Bible study. Clear and accurate charts and diagrams and a helpful glossary add value.

Ready to Grow
Practical steps to knowing God better

Alan Harkness

ISBN: 0 949720 71 2, **£5.99**

An attractive and practical book written to encourage believers to make time with God a regular part of their lives. Includes chapters on preparation, getting started, the practicalities, sharing what you have learned, and different methods of combining Bible reading and prayer.

Understanding the Bible

John Stott

ISBN 1 85999 225 0, £2.99

A special budget edition of a widely-acclaimed classic bestseller. Outstanding Christian teacher and author John Stott examines the cultural, social, geographical and historical background of the Bible, outlining the story and explaining the message.

A format pb 192pp

Understanding the Bible

John Stott

ISBN 1 85999 569 1, £9.99

A brand new edition in full colour. Revised and updated text is illustrated with charts, diagrams and wonderful colour photos. An ideal gift!

245x160mm hb 170pp

SMALL GROUP RESOURCES

Bodybuilders

A highly relational small group resource that's flexible and fun to use. Six outlines in each book contain notes for leaders, prayer and worship ideas, photocopiable sheets of interactive and in-depth Bible study material and ideas for personal study during the week.

A Fresh Encounter (David Bolster) 1 85999 586 1

**Designed for Great Things
(Anton Bauhmohl)** 1 85999 585 3

Living for the King ('Tricia Williams) 1 85999 584 5

Relationship Building (Lance Pierson) 1 85999 582 9

**Surviving Under Pressure (Christopher Griffiths &
Stephen Hathway)** 1 85999 587 X

Growing Through Change (Lance Pierson)
1 85999 583 7

210x140mm pb 32pp £3.50

Equipped for living

Florence MacKenzie

A series of four books designed for Christians wanting
in-depth Bible study in an engaging, personal style.
Thought-provoking questions for personal reflection and
application to life as well as for group discussion. Between
eight and ten studies in each book, illustrated by quotes from
a wide variety of authors.

**Living out the life of Jesus: The Fruit of the Spirit
1 85999 430 X**

**Living the kingdom lifestyle: The Beatitudes
1 85999 460 1**

**Living empowered for ministry:
The Gifts of the Spirit   1 85999 458 X**

**Living under God's protection: The Armour of God
1 85999 450**

4 All 210mmx40mm 80pp £3.50

Connect Bible Studies

Innovative, thought-provoking group Bible studies exploring key issues raised by contemporary films, TV programmes, books and music. Four weeks of material in each. Also available online: www.connectbiblestudies.com

Harry Potter   1 85999 578 0

The Matrix   1 85999 579 9

U2: 'All that you can't leave behind'   1 85999 580 2

Billy Elliot   1 85999 581 0

Chocolat   1 85999 608 6

TV Game Shows   1 85999 609 4

How to be Good   1 85999 610 8

Destiny's Child: 'Survivor'   1 85999 613 2

'AI': Artificial Intelligence   1 85999 626 4

Iris   1 85999 669 8

The Simpsons   1 85999 529 2

Dido: 'No Angel'   1 85999 679 5

The Lord of the Rings   1 85999 634 5

Sven: 'On Football'   1 85999 690 6

Superheroes   1 85999 702 3

All A4 24pp £3.00

For other resources, access our web site (www.scripture-union.,org.uk) or ring 01908 856006 to request our most up-to-date catalogues for Bible resources, church resources and children's ministry.